D1595065

Enamel
Medium for Fine Art

by
Margarete Seeler

DORRANCE PUBLISHING CO., INC.
PITTSBURGH, PENNSYLVANIA 15222

ISBN # 0-8059-3942-3
Library of Congress Catalog Card Number 96-084498
Printed in the United States of America

First Printing

For information or to order additional books, please write:
Dorrance Publishing Co., Inc.
643 Smithfield Street
Pittsburgh, Pennsylvania 15222
U.S.A.

In Memoriam

Hans Lehn

Table of Contents

Acknowledgments

My heartfelt thanks for cooperation to Alexandra Raphael, Theresa and Hans Zeitner, Professor Wolfgang Klose, George Hartley, Audrey Komrad, Joanne Conant and Tom Ellis.

Introduction

A lifetime of intense interest and learning has almost passed. Enamels of masters of times long ago, and my own errors and detours, taught me, as well as some youthful trying at the Berlin Academy of Fine and Applied Arts.

Years later the crucial inspiration took exactly one moment: Michael Wilm from Munich, the great goldsmith and master of enamelling, permitted me to hold a small Byzantine cloisonné enamel on gold in my hand; he did not know what happened, but my mind said, *This I understand, this I can do*. The spark has never died.

A word about the old controversy: What is *fine art* and what is *handcrafted art*?

I, for example, cannot see the difference between a good painted portrait (or a drawing), or one done in enamel. It cannot possibly be that the process of firing an enamelled portrait changes such a work into merely an object of decoration. The same holds for any composition of artistic value.

When I started to collect sketches and notes for this book, I wanted it to be quite matter of fact, with all my experiences available to those who might find them worthwhile. I will hold nothing back and I will speak in simple terms, without pretense, just reporting. Now the text being finished, I wish to emphasize that the "how to do it" is less important; it is the *why* which gives meaning to the objects. We must never forget that design, skill, and precious materials are only the vehicles that give lasting form to a thought.

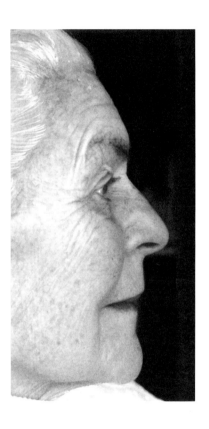

Chapter One
Basic Enamelling in a Nutshell

Since there are a great many books on the market which tell the story to the beginner, let me be as brief as possible. The word *enamel* signifies the finished object as well as the glassy material fused to a metal surface.

Raw Materials Needed

Enamel Colors

Enamel is finely ground special glass, tinted with metal oxides melting at similar temperatures. They come in three different melting points: soft, medium-hard, and hard and also can be transparent, opalescent, and opaque. Enamels can be purchased already ground to 60-80-mesh or in lumps. Lumps last almost forever and are ground when needed to be of perfect purity. When you buy your first set of enamels, transparents, opaques, and some flux, they will probably be all medium hard; that is fine for a limited number of layers fired on top of each other. One danger to remember is: Never wetpack a hard enamel over a soft one. The layers do not fuse properly, causing horizontal cracks. Hard is to be used first; the medium hard on top; and the soft will fill deep areas or produce the last fine hues of color.

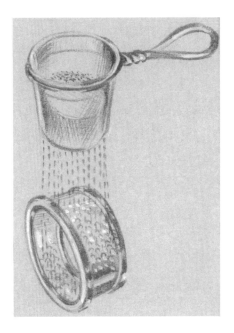

Glue

Binders like agar or tragacanth (Klyr-Fire) hold sifted enamel in place. It is not necessary on flat surfaces. If we have a curved or vertical piece, we spray Klyr-Fire first, sift, spray again, and sift again—up to three times, so that a solid coat of two to three layers covers the metal surface before the first firing. Sift thinly.

Small pinches of enamel are held between thumb and index finger and sliding along the rim of the piece, sprinkled as a heavy rim.

The last layer will be glue. The rims may need a bit of special care (see illustration).

What Klyr-Fire can do for us on a non-flat but very vertical surface which is completely covered with glued-on cloisons will be explained in the description of the enamelled chalice in Chapter Ten. The wires and the enamel were all applied at the same time, all around the cup...quite a challenging and also inspiring task.

Flux

Flux is a colorless first coating which is necessary on copper in order to achieve brilliant colors. It should be sifted just thick enough to cover the surface well; a bit heavier around the edges. When fired really high, it turns to a beautiful golden transparent color.

For work on silver, flux #2A Schauer or Thompson #1209 are safe and clear. One needs flux under reds, oranges, pinks, and some purples; everything else is good without flux when working on pure silver, and a bit less brilliant on sterling silver and sterling silver casts.

Fire samples first as it saves a lot of nerves and time.

Transparent Enamels

I suggest buying them in lumps and grinding them as they are needed. It takes only minutes to prepare the small amounts that one uses for each job. If, however, the finished piece is to be large, ground transparents may be freely sifted. If flawless clarity is essential, one must wash the powdered enamel until all whitish silt is gone. Then dry it in a tray lined with paper towel, and put it in a very warm place: on top of the kiln, or for faster results, into an oven with the door left open.

Grinding lumps is done in a hard porcelain or agate mortar with a porcelain pestle with a wooden handle. Do not use too many lumps at a time and cover them with water. Guide the pestle over the lumps, hitting it with controlled, sharp strokes with a hammer. Soon the lumps will be small enough to permit grinding by hand to uniformly small grains. The sound will tell how fine it is. Then wash the silt off, renewing the water several times. The enamel is now ready to be wetpacked into its final place. It looks most appetizing and a tray with all the colors needed puts the mind into that relaxed state so necessary for good work.

Opalescent Enamels

Opalescent enamels are semi-transparent, a bit like milky glass. When used in the normal manner they fire beautifully. There are rather demanding ways to change the opalescents into a two-color reflecting appearance: This is achieved by submitting them to several firings at different temperatures. On copper, tombac, and gold without flux, fire hot first until the opalescent becomes opaque. Fire again at approximately 1300 degrees (704 degrees Celsius), and check when the opalescent effect appears. Pink opalescents on silver need flux. Repeat both firings if necessary.

Opaque Enamels

Opaque enamels can be used as bought, ground to 80-mesh. Wash just the quantity you need; they will fire nice and even. For large, decorative pieces washing is not necessary if the colors are relatively fresh and kept in closed jars. Old enamels can be restored by washing and grinding and discarding all the whitish silt.

Methods of Application

Sifting

Sifting is done nicely and evenly with sieves, either over the whole surface or with different colors over stencils.

Wetpacking

Wetpacking means to apply the moist-to-wet, ground enamel with a good brush or a tiny metal spoon, spreading it evenly. A ripple-tool passed along the rim, tapping from underneath, or gently knocking it on a hard base brings the water to the surface where it can be soaked up with a paper tissue or a strip of clean cotton. A very simple tool made from a pencil pushes the grains of enamel into smallest places, packing it tightly, and making the surface even.

WOOD

PORCELAIN

LUMPS

AGATE

FOR FINE GRINDING

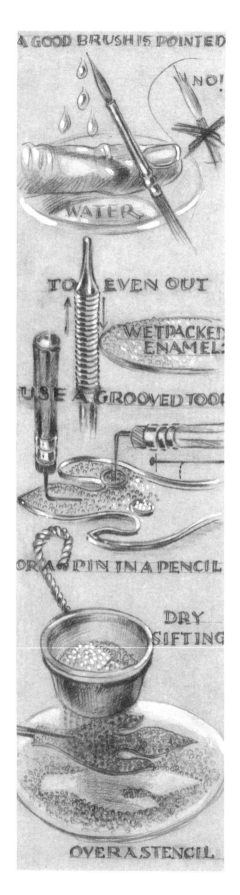

A GOOD BRUSH IS POINTED

NO!

WATER

TO EVEN OUT

WETPACKED ENAMEL

USE A GROOVED TOOL

OR A PIN IN A PENCIL

DRY SIFTING

OVER A STENCIL

Coating

The insides of three-dimensional objects which cannot be reached otherwise should be partly filled with a creamy mix of glue and enamel and by turning the object in all directions, a coating with counter enamel is achieved.

Painting

Grisaille

Grisaille is an extremely fine-ground white powder which can be applied with water, but it is better when ground with a very small amount of thick oil of turpentine on a piece of glass with a spatula.

Different oils are used as thinners, each affecting the reaction of the grisaille while working. Turpentine will make sharp contours possible while oil of cloves or lavender lets the grisaille flow (see Chapters Ten and Twenty-three).

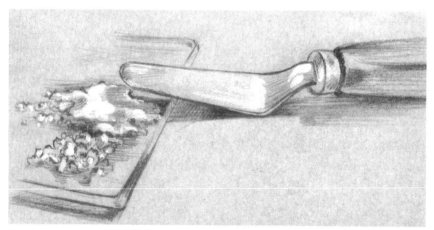

Enamel Painting Colors

I am far from suggesting china-painting on enamel, but there are times when it is good to be familiar with it. These enamel-painting colors are finely ground; they are prepared for work similar to grisaille and are dried and fired in the same manner. If you are a painter, you will find some very exciting applications of these colors as sharp line designs between areas of transparents or opaque enamel. The firing must be low (1300 degrees Fahrenheit). Compare grisaille.

Fine Gold and Fine Silver Fired Over Enamel

Fine gold and fine silver painted as finishing touches over grisaille enamel is beautiful. This technique should be used with restraint. The gold is known to the refiner as *sponge* and to the china-painter as *Roman gold*. It is ground extremely fine, then mixed like grisaille with thick oil of turpentine. The application has to be quite thick. Fire until barely glowing; then remove the piece and check to see if a pointed tool can still remove the gold. It must have fused to the enamel. If so, polish the piece with a burnisher, or it can remain matte if treated with a glass brush under running water.

Underglazes

These are colors painted directly on the metal, dried, coated with sifted transparents, and fired. I use Underglaze D which remains black. If the design should turn invisible in the finished piece, I draw with a black Stabilo All 8046. On copper it changes to a very light transparent.

When to Counter Enamel?

Should one counter enamel after the front has one coat of enamel fired to it, or before the front is done?

On Copper

If the front is to be very clear, I like to take into account the doming which takes place by itself when you enamel the front first. The back is protected by Scalex. Counter enamel in the next firing. A domed piece may be enamelled on both sides at the same time: spray glue; sift; spray glue again; sift, and last, spray.

On Sterling Silver

First, a neat counter enamel with transparents which looks good directly on silver is advisable. Pickle the piece, engrave, or finish the front with a diamond wheel in order to enhance reflection and to give more hold to the enamel.

Sterling Casts: Enamel the back first. No oxidation appears on the front as long as the whitish coating is not damaged.

On Fine Silver

Fine silver cannot oxidize. Counter enamel first, so that you do not have to be concerned with it any more, then proceed with the front.

On Gold

Fine gold needs no flux. N-T gold needs flux only under red, pink, and orange.

The back should be treated with the same care as the front. Enamelling the back first makes working on the front much easier.

Band Rings (gold or silver)

Enamel both sides at the same time, using suitable transparents.

Tall Vertical Shapes (Foot of a Chalice)

Enamel the outside first, using flux, since it is elastic and will not crack. If a dark color is desired, mix the flux with the color in equal parts. Use Scalex on the inside if the shape is copper. Fire and, after it cools, clean and coat the inside with a creamy mix of glue and flux, or spray and sift alternately. Places that cannot be reached with the sieves are *salted* by hand. Be sure that enough Klyr-Fire has been sprayed and respray if necessary to hold the counter enamel solidly. It is possible to fire this counter enamel simultaneously with the front.

Red Enamels and Some Tricky Opaques

All red enamels demand our special attention.

Opaque reds directly on copper are no problem. They fire perfectly even and are beautiful. But use the same red without flux on silver and it will turn out with black rims and black spots. In cloisonné work, the coat of flux or white under the red should be thin; otherwise you might stone through the red and end up with red-spotted flux or white enamel. Still, when using silver, it is hard to avoid the small black rim around each red area; more precisely, it cannot be avoided. At times, however, it can be rather attractive.

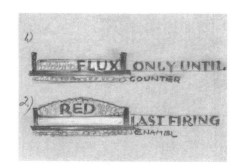

Transparent reds are a real problem. They should be ground coarser than other colors for best transparency.

On copper, if fired only once, some are extremely beautiful. To prevent flux from firing through in small golden dots, mix one-half flux and one-half red for the first coat. Then add the second coat of red and the result will be good. If the piece has many colors, complete it except for the areas where the transparent red is to go. There, leave just the flux over the copper. Add the reds before the last firing, which should be quick and high.

When you work with silver, use the proper flux for the alloy. Again, add the reds at the last firing. Reds become brownish when fired too often. No problems exist with red transparents directly on gold. No flux is necessary. This means that you can get the perfect red on any metal if you underlay with gold, either a very thin-rolled gold sheet, which will not wrinkle, or foil, which will wrinkle.

Pink transparents are even worse than reds. After the first firing they are as gentle as pink can be. Fire them again and they turn into a bluish, dark pink. On copper they should be fired over opaque white and again only once or twice at most. Over gold, pinks are delightful, but they change to orange-pink. Cover a pink with opal white as a last coat and only poetry can describe the result. Some seashells have such hues on the inside.

White, of course, is opaque except for opal white. It is affected by acids and becomes dull. Soft white fired very high directly on copper without flux turns into a very beautiful gold, green, and brown where the heat began to eat it away. This could be an inspiring background (for gold cloisonné) if very light transparents are used in a free and imaginative manner.

Opaque white should be ground very finely for greater density. If a white-enamelled piece turns yellow around the edges, it was overfired.

Black opaque is best fired only once. It, too, does not agree with acid. To get a spotlessly clean black is no easy task. Ground from lumps is the safest way.

If opaques appear dull, they have either been in a kiln at too low a temperature for too long, or they have been exposed to acid or pickle, or the enamel was old and not washed.

Metal Bases for Enamelling

Copper

Copper is excellent for large objects. Copper needs flux and counter enamel. If only opaques are used, flux is not necessary. Copper takes high heat without melting, but it tarnishes badly and forms thick copper-scale. Under very high-fired flux this irregular scale can produce quite interesting effects. If one is not aiming for such *lucky accidents*, Scalex should be painted over all copper parts which are not covered with enamel. The Scalex comes off together with the layer of oxidation when the piece cools, but one must watch and remove every trace of it; it causes black spots in the fired enamel, which can only be removed by grinding them out, refilling the indentation and refiring. What a job that is!

Silver

Fine silver (1000/1000) is pure without alloys. It enamels very well but is too soft for objects in daily use.

Sterling silver (935/1000) contains 65 parts of alloys; mostly copper. It, too, is good for enameling if immaculately clean. The result is not quite as brilliant as on fine silver. It tarnishes on those parts which hold no enamel. Therefore, I suggest finishing the bare metal parts to perfection **before** the last firing. Every scratch is a hiding place for oxidation. When all enamelling is done, immerse the piece in lukewarm Sparex; it comes out neat and white.

There are very few enamels that cannot take Sparex. Black and White get dull, so cover them with a bit of asphaltum or wax before Sparex-cleaning. When polishing the piece, it is wise to cover the enamelled parts with masking tape, so that a file or an abrasive can do no damage. Silver **needs** counter enamel. It expands in the kiln; the enamel runs over the expanded surface which becomes smaller when cooling, and that means cracks and distortion. Counter enamel leaves only one direction for the silver to expand—sideways. That is why enamels *grow* in the kiln and will not fit into a prepared bezel. Finish the enamel first, then make the bezel.

Cast Silver

It works very well if the metal construction—the model—provides protection on all sides for the enamel.

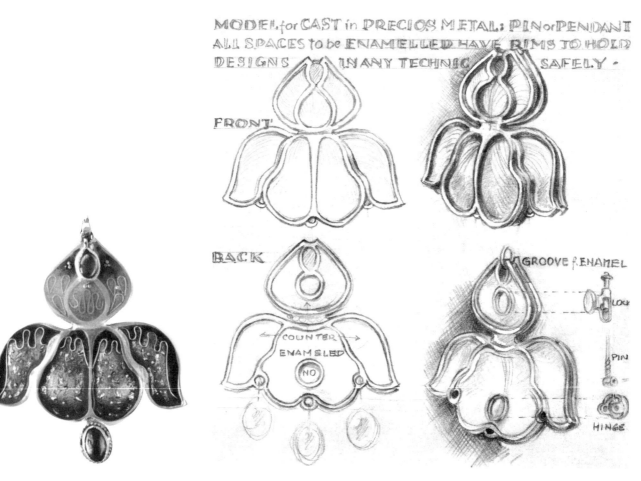

MODEL for CAST in PRECIOS METAL; PIN or PENDANT
ALL SPACES to be ENAMELLED HAVE RIMS TO HOLD
DESIGNS — IN ANY TECHNIC — SAFELY —

FRONT

BACK

COUNTER
ENAMELED
NO

GROOVE f. ENAMEL
LOCK
PIN
HINGE

The casts should not be porous, which means a good caster has to make them; and they must have a white coating (which happens by itself).

The model has a space for counter enamel, for hinges, or for places to add fittings later on. It is advisable to think ahead about all possibilities of the use the cast may have built in, and the enameller only needs to remove the sprues and other details which will not be used. On these spots the sterling silver will tarnish during firings. The rest of the cast will stay white and clean.

For enamelling, remove the white coat only on those places which are to receive enamel in the very next firing. To get more brilliancy and a better hold, use a Florentine graving tool or just a dentist's burr to roughen the surface and increase reflection. No white coating is to be overlooked! Before the first firing, polish the bare silver inside and outside to perfection. As mentioned before: Less oxidation can occur on a flawless surface than on one which has scratches and uneven areas. Clean the piece well, (no traces of polishing rouge should remain), dry it, and if there are tiny low spots left in the enamel, fill them with just the right amount of either clear soft flux on light colors, or transparents on the dark ones (a lighter transparent shade than the underlying color though). Let dry with a bit of Klyr-Fire on top, so the grains of enamel will not jump inside the kiln or melt onto the silver.

The last firing should be high and fast. You get the finest surface this way. But beware of over-firing: The silver may melt and then you are left with something really ugly, black, and irreparable. A quick bath in Sparex or acid and cleaning with a glass brush—maybe some polishing—is all that is needed to finish the work. Such casts have one great advantage: no discoloration of the enamel from solder.

Gold

Gold is ideal and without problems when it is pure. It needs no counter enamel, and all colors come out perfect, except for the color of the gold tinting the transparents. Blues become turquoisey, greens are deep and beautiful, and reds are unsurpassed. But pure gold is very soft and the finished pieces should be treated like precious stones; They should be set deep into protective bezels and not be exposed to wear and tear.

There is one kind of 18-carat gold—I call it N-T (non tarnishing) gold—which consists of 750 parts fine gold and 250 parts fine silver. It does not tarnish, costs less than fine gold, is lighter in color, quite soft, and enamels very well. For rings N-T gold might wear too fast; for everything else it will do perfectly. But remember that it contains silver; therefore, one must put a coat of flux under those spots which are to be red, pink, orange, or purple.

Gilder's Metal

This metal, also called Tombac, is a copper alloy. It casts very well, but should contain no more than three or four percent zinc. If it is enamelled it can be gold plated; it is inexpensive and good for the production of many pieces. Underlay transparents with gold or silver foil or thin sheet, which first is fired over flux. It must have counter enamel unless the object is very thick and the enamel very thin. When using gilder's metal, one should apply as few coats of enamel and fire as few times as possible.

Steel and Aluminum

They can be enamelled but that is outside the scope of this book.

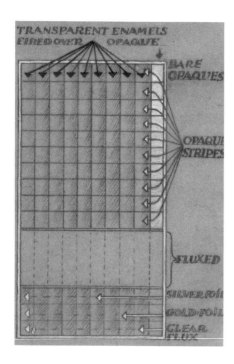

The Sample Plaque

Why don't you begin by making a sample plaque:

For the experienced craftsperson as well as the beginner, samples of all the colors are essential to show what a wealth of shades even a small number of opaques and transparents on different backgrounds produce. A copper panel of four-inch-by-six-inch, eighteen gauge (1 millimeter) will suffice.

1. Start by shaping the plaque properly, edges bent down. Clean the surface in Sparex. Then brush under running water with a glass brush, never with steel wool. Steel wool has no place in the enamelling shop. It is greasy and leaves small particles of iron which contaminate enamels and the work area.

2. Scratch strong lines vertically and horizontally into the plaque with a scriber. You need vertical lines where the opaques are to be applied, and as many horizontals as you have enamels. These lines will remain visible under a coat of copper flux.

3. Paint Scalex over the front and the very left strip, let dry and generously sift counter enamel on the back. Fire. Immerse the cooled piece into a Sparex bath (warm works faster) and clean it very well with a glass brush under running water.

As a next step, an even coat of flux is sifted over the front with the incised lines, except for the very left strip which remains bare. The Scalex on this strip is to be painted anew before firing the flux high to golden clarity.

We are now ready to sift a hard opaque white over the designated area and glue the strips of silver and gold foil into their places (the foil is cut between layers of tissue paper and gently lifted with tweezers). When dry and covered with tissue paper, one can rub it tightly to the flux.

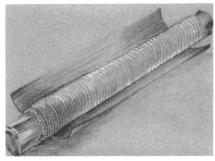

Glass brush

4. Wetpack all opaque enamels onto the vertical strips, let dry, and fire. It is all right to fire the foil together with the opaques. Once these are fired, a second layer of all transparents is wetpacked horizontally over the opaques, gold, silver, and white. Only on top, or as the last line, the opaques remain uncovered. One sample plaque of that kind shows us hundreds of variations of twenty to thirty different enamel colors. If done with care, it is a showpiece in the shop. Many craftspeople fire small samples of each color and attach them individually to the bottle containing the enamel, or they invent a system which lets them choose the right color from single samples one-inch square. I personally would miss the many variations of one color and opportunity to select from the entire range of possibilities.

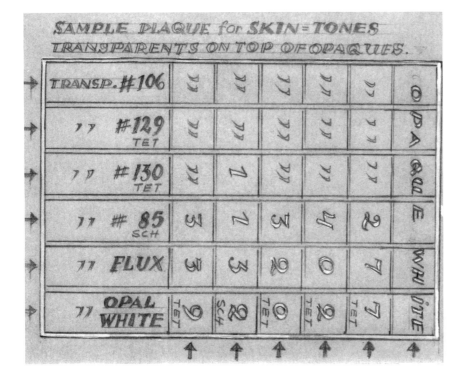

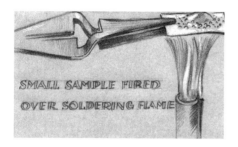

SMALL SAMPLE FIRED
OVER SOLDERING FLAME

Special Sample for Important Work

Even if the craftsperson knows the colors by heart and knows what they can do, it is wise to have special samples for each task to make sure that the colors will be in harmony with each other; that they have the same melting points; and that they will achieve the desired effect on the metal intended for use.

Samples of Skin Shades

A three-inch-by-three-inch square of copper is large enough for a sample.

Counter enamel after the front has received a coat of flux, then wetpack vertical strips of all the ivory, tan, beige, and light brown opaques you have. Fire these to maturity. Over these verticals, wetpack strips of all fine transparent grays, tan, light brown, brown-olive, etc., and fire again. When you realize that a final coat of clear flux will draw the harshness of colors together and blend them harmoniously, you have a nice palette for figure and portrait enamelling.

Chapter Two
Tools

Trivets

Trivets are ugly, dark-stained, distorted, and abused, yet utterly useful and patient things. Suppliers have some useful trivets, but for the special object to be put into the glowing-hot kiln safely and without touching the enamel at any spot, one is better to bend a trivet to shape from wire mesh or stainless steel bands.

Since a well-planned piece has rims or metal wherever the trivet holds it, it is indeed fun to invent useful trivets from anything.

It is most important that the enamelled piece rests well on the trivet; it should have no chance to slide or lose its shape. In order to clean trivets, scrape the edges with a sharp file, hammer splatter off, or drop them hot into cold water...they take it!

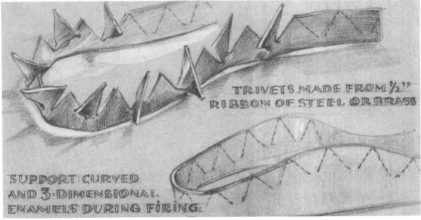

TRIVETS MADE FROM ½" RIBBON OF STEEL OR BRASS

SUPPORT CURVED AND 3-DIMENSIONAL ENAMELS DURING FIRING.

About Firing

Concentrate! Do not talk! Hold your breath for a moment and do it carefully, without losing your balance or dropping the piece inside the kiln. If it happens, think first, and then maneuver it out with firing forks and a long spatula. If the kiln door opens downward, rest the rod of the firing fork carefully on the open door front, and then slowly let the fork part with the trivet and your work inside the kiln. In this manner you avoid any shock. The procedure is quick and not too much heat is lost. Any opening of the kiln should be done fast since the temperature drops 100 degrees or more at once.

There is no rule for firing times. However, if you have to repeat a piece and wish to eliminate the guesswork, take notes on the time to fire and the temperature which produced the best result.

While the plaque is still in the kiln, observe it and remove the piece when the enamel has fused to an even, shiny surface. If the enamel is underfired, the surface still looks like "orange peel" and the transparents are dull. If cloisonné is underfired, the colors will creep to the middle of the cells, away from the rims, or cloisons. Tarnishing metals will get dark, but if you put the piece right back into the kiln immediately and refire it, the enamel will smooth out.

If fired at a rather high temperature, the enamel will creep up the sides of the rims, or cloisons. If you overheat silver and silver cloisons, they disappear into the enamel, melt over the copper base, or turn into very ugly black lumps. Such a piece cannot be saved. It happens to all of us until we know better.

Never remove a hot piece from the trivet forcibly. If it is stuck to the trivet, wait for a few minutes. If you tear it off, the hot enamel will be torn off too, forming long threads of glass from the piece and leaving bare spots. Left alone to cool, it will come off the trivet easily by itself and leave only tiny marks. If the metal was preshaped, as suggested in most of these chapters, you will never run into this problem. There is always a clean metal edge on which the piece can rest.

If you fire very large plaques with complicated details, and it is not possible to bend the rims down on the copper, there is a danger that they will not stay completely flat.

My method of precaution is:

1. The wire mesh trivet is as even as a hammer on a steel anvil can flatten it. Then I cover it with **mica** to prevent the counter enamel from sticking.

2. I keep a hot steel plate with a strong handle on top of my kiln.

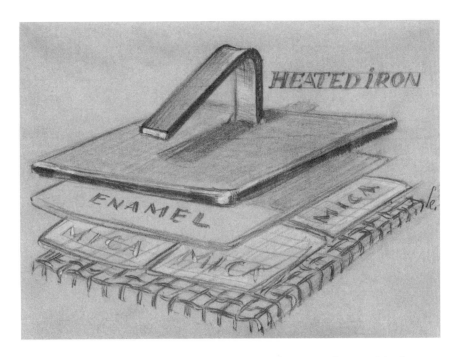

3. The moment when I take the trivet with the enamel out of the heat, it still glows red. I place this hot steel plate on top of it and press where it might need it. There it stays until I need it for the next plaque.

4. If several such large plaques are to be fired, I have a second set of all these tools and go on firing. (For example the ten plaques for the altar in Chapter Twenty-eight.)

5. I always work on two plaques at the same time. While one cools, the other is wetpacked, dried, and ready to be fired.

Tools needed

Of course one needs a *kiln*, and it would be better to have two of them. One should be very small but of good quality for firing quick samples or tiny objects, and the larger kiln should be at least eight-inches-by-eight-inches and four-to-five-inches high inside the firing chamber, depending upon the work that is to be done.

The enamels are kept in *glass jars* indicating the number, the producer's name, the degree of hardness, and whether they are *opaque* or *transparent* on the label. To keep them arranged by number makes it easier to find them. One may glue a sample of the fired color on the jar, but experience shows that after very little time one knows the qualities of each enamel so well that it seems unnecessary, and the sample plaque holds all the information anyway. If the enameller is a silver or goldsmith and wants enamel in small amounts on his work, he can fire instant samples over the flame of a torch, enamelling on a snip of metal held with a pair of tweezers. Such samples are good enough to show results, although perishable since no counter enamel is used.

I keep my assortment of enamels for daily use in white *plastic spoons* which are covered when not in use—if they were not so easily available someone would have to invent them!

You will also need a *sawframe* and blades—0.3 blades for thick metal.

The small *pliers* for bending cloisonné wires should be watchmaker's pliers of the best quality. File them down in such a manner that you will need only one tool for every possible shape to be bent: One jaw should remain flat inside, but the sides should be filed to sharp 90 degree angles. The other jaw should be filed to a tapered, round shape. The jaws must touch when the pliers are closed.

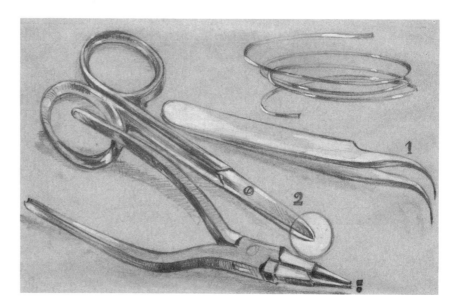

Buff and polish the pliers with as much care as you would a piece of fine jewelry. They must feel like a part of your hand and turn easily to any necessary position. The rectangular tip is for bending sharp corners, and the round tip is for making small circles and to hold the wire for making gentle curves.

You also need:

1. One pair of small watchmaker's tweezers.
2. A fine pair of small scissors, which must cut at the very tip.
3. One good sable brush, either #0 or #1.
4. Small white plastic spoons.
5. Three glasses for water, waste, and washing the brush.
6. Klyr-Fire or tragacanth (binders which do not decompose for some time and fire away completely).
7. Several pieces of mica.
8. Trivets to hold the piece in the kiln, and tongs to place the work in the kiln and remove it.

9. A couple of sieves, which you can buy or make yourself.
10. An old surgical tool with a rippled handle. This tool is passed over the edge of the piece after wetpacking. The vibration smooths the enamel and lets the moisture come to the surface where it can easily be absorbed with tissue paper.
11. Distilled water, though clean well water will also do.
12. If you plan to do very fine work, you should have magnifying eyeglasses.
13. A pencil with india rubber and a bent pin.
14. Lastly, it is most comfortable to place your piece on a small wooden block covered with paper towel which you can turn around, thus reaching the work from all sides without moving it from its rest.

15. A wooden mallet, one side softened with a piece of leather tied over it.

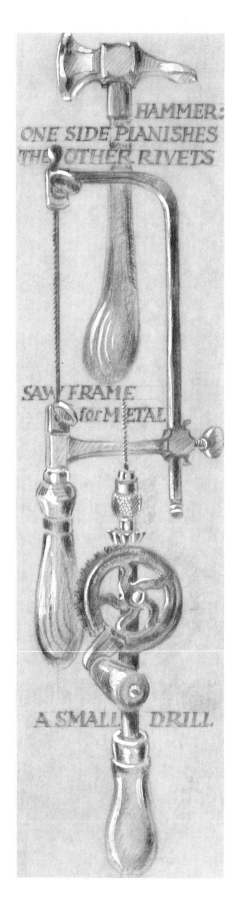

HAMMER:
ONE SIDE PLANISHES
THE OTHER RIVETS

SAW FRAME
for METAL

A SMALL DRILL.

Nice-to-have-tools

16. A flexible shaft with drills, burrs, polishing wheels, diamond-impregnated wheels, etc.
17. A thermostat for your kiln.
18. A small vice and some stakes to shape metal.
19. A polished planishing hammer.
20. Used x-ray film from a hospital's x-ray laboratory. It is ideal to use for models to construct three-dimensional metal shapes.
21. A good compass and a surface gauge to control the evenness of heights.

That is about it. Add never-ending patience and let me whisper a helpful word in your ears: When you have bad luck, say to yourself: *I did it once, I can do it again.*

Chapter Three
Byzantine Metal Shapes Ready for Enamelling without Soldering

At the doorstep of the Middle Ages there was Byzantium. Rome had decayed and with that, the Dark Ages fell over Western Europe. The Eastern Roman Empire had become a Christian theocracy; a new way of thought and of life emerged, which was based upon the imperial power structure of Rome. All gold belonged to the emperor, whose power was very close to that of God. The new religion needed new cult objects which represented or held what was sacred. Oriental and Greek artisans were available and gold was plentiful. Democracies rarely concentrate such wealth in one hand. It takes either an almost God-like ruler, or it is done for the glory of God. Both ask for utterly devoted men or slaves: Look at Egypt, ancient China, Etruria, the medieval cathedrals...or Byzantium.

At one time in Munich, Professor Doctor Brunner (head of the Schatz-kammer and a fine artist-goldsmith himself) and I wondered how, in the old Byzantine cloisonnés, the spaces to hold the enamel had been set so evenly deep. He suggested with punches. However, in my own studio I had experimented and found another way. I showed him the result of my experiment.

I had produced the tool for the top of a swivel ring which I had made in the manner which, I think, the Byzantine craftsmen used. Professor Doctor Brunner was interested enough in my method and together we went to take the *Goldene Tafel* out of its glass case.

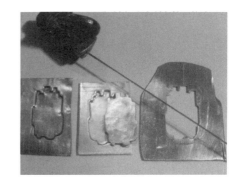

The *Goldene Tafel* was a center piece of a large book cover or part of an altar. It was made in Byzantium in 1200 A.D., and is 18.5 centimeters high, I guess, the gold being about 1/2 millimeter thick.

It is not counter enamelled. In its lower left corner there is a soldier's shield, which has a sharp cut through the gold where the enamel begins. I suggested that this was proof for my experiment, and that what I call *tool and die* (T&D) had been used.

Professor Doctor Brunner and I had become friends over our mutual love and respect for the old masters. He agreed with my ideas.

Take a piece of eighteen gauge copper or bronze. Draw on it the exact outline of the part to hold enamel cloisons. Drill one or two small openings to barely admit the sawblade. The width of the sawblade should correspond to the thickness of the precious metal sheet to be used. Saw slowly, carefully, and avoid corners that are too intricate or shapes that are too slim because the metal may not stretch this much (gold does amazingly well) without being damaged.

You now have two pieces: one with an opening and one which fits into that opening. File gently around both, break the edges, hold it against the light, and see if the distance of the inner and outer piece are evenly wide all around. Fits that are too tight have the effect of scissors (see the *Goldene Tafel*).

The round design simplifies understanding and the choice of shapes is unlimited as long as they are not overstretching the metal. A good example to show what should not be done is the snowflake. The size of the tiny Pegasus made of twenty-two carat gold (one inch by one and one-half inches) is about the limit.

FILE

SAW

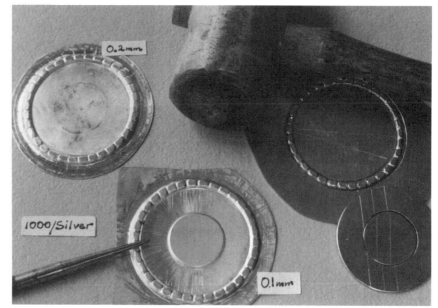

0.2 mm

1000/Silver

0.1 mm

The only indispensable skill is sawing. The beaded ring is twice as thick as the flat copper. I soldered a second sheet of copper underneath. This beaded ring gives incredible stiffness even to very thin metal. The center may provide space for a stone or, if set deep, space for an enamel.

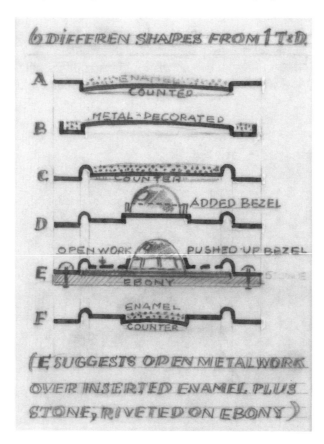

6 DIFFEREN SHAPES FROM 1 T&D.

A ENAMEL
COUNTER

B METAL-DECORATED

C COUNTER

D ADDED BEZEL

OPEN WORK   PUSHED UP BEZEL

E EBONY

F ENAMEL
COUNTER

(E SUGGESTS OPEN METALWORK
OVER INSERTED ENAMEL PLUS
STONE, RIVETED ON EBONY)

When all parts are filed and fitted, assemble them and scribe differing witness marks over both sides in order to always know what goes where. Now put the piece with the opening on a flat anvil and lay your thin sheet of gold or silver over the opening. I use thicknesses of about 0.15 millimeter for fine silver and 0.07 to 0.1 millimeter for gold, depending on size. The metal is annealed. Press with your thumb over the opening and you will see the indentation quite clearly in the precious metal sheet. With a small paper mallet, or a wooden one over which a piece of leather is tied to soften the blows, gently sharpen the edges.

Shows the T&D used in two directions

The background is set deep

T&D makes it possible to raise the enamelled design above the flat metal.

The design is set deep

The finished piece

The copper parts also serve as stencils. Painted with Scalex, to prevent oxidation, they also avoid warpage during and after firing, if placed underneath the object to be enamelled.

Insert the other part of the T&D exactly, cover with a piece of hard wood, and hammer the insert down. In less than one minute the shape is ready for enamelling. Sometimes you may wish to sharpen the edges slightly: Do it extremely gently with a polished planishing hammer—more rubbing than striking. If hit too hard, the copper stretches and the tool becomes too tight. With one T&D one can easily produce six to ten imprints. The same applies to more intricate forms.

Using it the other side up, you have two differing shapes, and if you enamel the background and keep the inner part raised, you have four different possibilities from the same T&D.

But that is not all: Our T&D serves us when the enamelled pieces are inserted into the kiln and the question of the correct trivet comes up. Just paint part of your T&D with Scalex, cover with mica, and the piece rests perfectly flat on it and on a mica-covered wire mesh trivet.

It is safe and easy. The same holds when polishing on a wheel: Put the T&D over a piece of hard board, the cloisonné enamel on top, and go ahead. Our colleagues from Byzantium must have had substantial manufactures to provide European courts, monasteries, and cathedrals with their artifacts. I guess they worked on a kind of conveyer belt, some bent the shapes of wire—boxes full of the same—some set them, others filled in the enamels. Probably one color at a time, and so on. Hands and faces were reserved for the more skillful. The gowns and so on were covered with identical repetitions of small shapes, many easily formed over sticks of hardwood.

But alas...the men who designed and made the prototypes—what dignity and expression on a few square centimeters! There were no drawplates and no rolling mills, but legions of cheap labor, and they knew how to beat natural gold extremely thin. For me, the simplest way to make cloisonné wire is to cut the annealed thin gold sheet into strips 0.8 millimeters wide—no loss, no complicated tools. The miles of flat wire, very thin, must have been made in a similar manner.

To straighten this wire I use my fingertips; fingernails already harden it.

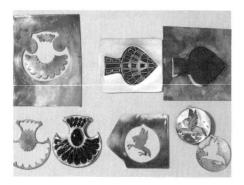
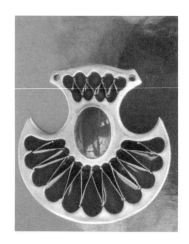

Chapter Four
Low Reliefs for Multiple Reproductions from Metal

This chapter follows logically the previously discussed T&D technique which provided metal backgrounds with low elevations only.

Art historians tell us that in the sixteenth century in France, the raised effects of limoge enamels were achieved by firing layer upon layer of opaque flesh-tones; only in the last firing a painted-on dark enamel for contours and pure gold for fine lines and details was used, these two having a much lower melting point.

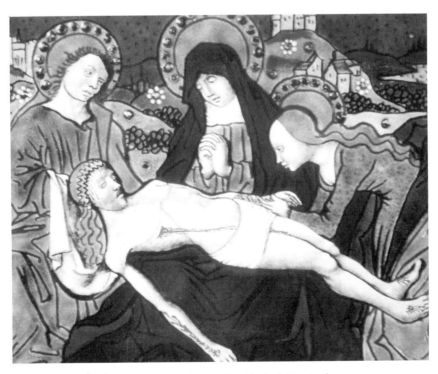

Medieval French Limoges—painted enamel with slightly raised parts.

The French masters must have had opaques different from ours. I fear it would not work with today's material.

To achieve the same results with today's enamel colors—and to be able to multiply such an object of art—you need a T&D, using only the open part of it. Here is a safe way:

When the design is reduced to the few critical lines, paint a piece of copper sheet of twenty gauge with white tempera. It should be two inches wider than your drawing. Let it dry and trace your design onto it. Now incise it with a sharp point through the white, or use an electric hand engraver. Wash the white off and saw out those areas which will be slightly domed.

For limoge we put the thin sheet of metal to become enamelled over the holes of our T&D, and very gently press this metal into the openings. **No sharp contours**—only light indentations, respectively with **elevations** on the side to be enamelled.

T&D   Raised from the back   Painted in Limoges manner

The back receives its coat of counter enamel; the front is covered with high-fired flux, and you are ready to freely add foil, paint, wetpack, fire, and repeat these processes until all colors are right. Figures and/or heads are still just domed opaque. Only now add the design with either fine-line black, or any oil-based china paint.

The best sable brush is just good enough. Shading with painting enamels and/or gold—all these last touches are done before the next and last firing, which is much lower than firings before.

For such limoge enamels, I highly recommend providing a rim which is not enamelled and may be bent down to a boxlike shape. It prevents warping and allows a clean counter enamel and easy setting of the finished plaque, which can be screwed to a wood or metal frame from the inside of the back.

I can imagine triptychs—I see the tops and sides of precious boxes, and single plaques, learning from the old, but using themes of today and tomorrow.

A geometrical, rather simple relief has been made with an eighteen gauge thick T&D. It may be used positive or negative, hold enamel or stones, or both. The extended use of such a T&D is shown in Chapter Nineteen.

Very thin gold—0.09 millimeters thick—permits very detailed reproductions over a small sculptured head. It is to be filled evenly in the back with a two-component epoxy, which hardens to keep the shape, and which can be filed and sanded. Only a wooden tool is used at the beginning and when nearly completed a polished burnisher will give it the final sharpness. If N-T gold is used, such a piece can be well enamelled. The counter enamel, which is to fill the sculpture from the back, will give it protection against distortion.

MODEL

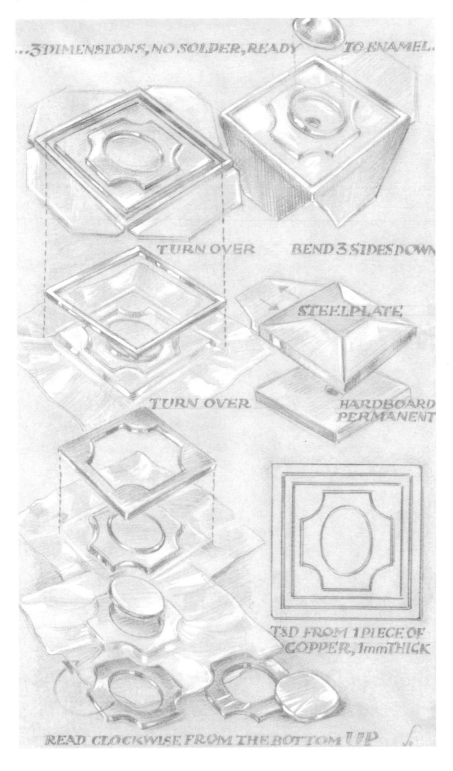

...3 DIMENSIONS, NO SOLDER, READY TO ENAMEL.

TURN OVER   BEND 3 SIDES DOWN

STEELPLATE

TURN OVER   HARDBOARD PERMANENT

T&D FROM 1 PIECE OF COPPER, 1mm THICK

READ CLOCKWISE FROM THE BOTTOM UP

Chapter Five
Low Reliefs for Multiple Reproduction over Hard-Fired Porcelain

Chasing a delicate design into thin, precious metal is a skill which few enamellers master.

Here is a way to produce such reliefs: The inspiration came from antique Greek jewels where small golden heads of humans and/or animals are part of gold-granulated masterpieces. Archeologists think that the Greek rubbed thin gold over carved hardwood or stone. To achieve a sculpture in the round, halves or parts were joined together, probably in the same manner used to hold gold granulation on their bases. Welding without solder we might call it. The result was a hollow shape. I do not know what the ancient goldsmiths filled it with to avoid distortion but I use a two-component epoxy which hardens and can be filed and drilled like wood. I cannot carve wood. For many years I have searched for a way how we today, could create rock hard small sculptures. I found one and will share it with you:

Negative Cutting in Plaster of Paris:

1. Coat a glass slab thinly with Vaseline, without leaving any trace of finger prints. Build a rim of plasticene, comfortably large enough for the plaster that you will work on. This rim should be not less than one and one-half-inches high.

2. Mix plaster of Paris water first, and then loosely and slowly sift the dry powder into the water, until a small hill is not soaked up. Make more than you think you will need.

3. Stir gently. If you want softer casts, stir a bit more and pour one-third of the thickness that you want into the plasticene wall. Knock on the underside of the glass slab so that all the air bubbles rise; then fill in the rest. Knock the slab again and leave it alone.

4. When the plaster has hardened, remove the plasticene rim and push the plaster off the glass. Give it a day or more to dry.

5. You are now ready to apply your design very sparingly—not deep, just visible—with a soft pencil.

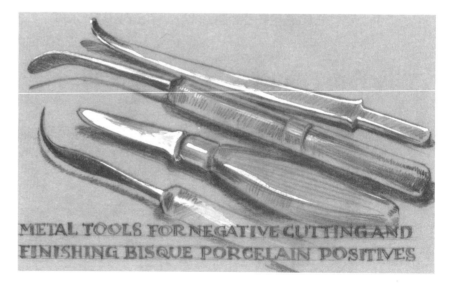

The tools you need are tools one cannot buy, but must make just right for the task. Small knives, spatulas that have been bent to the appropriate shape, manicure tools, all **metal**, polished and very sharp.

Now cut **negative** while, in your spare hand, you hold a blob of plasticene to make imprints and check the positive effect. It takes a bit of brain gymnastics to remember to *cut deep what is to be high*.

Let me continue the procedure with a natural shell (1). It has been reduced to the shape I am aiming for (2), and has been cast as negative in plaster of Paris.

Do not coat with shellac—that is only done for castings in plaster—**but make several imprints with porcelain**, that white, fine, moist, buttery material which will come out as perfect positive images of the negative-cut plaster.

Let dry for a day or two and use your metal tools again to work over this porcelain as far as possible. You take away, you put a drop of water where you need to add, and add with a small spatula or brush. Dry thoroughly and trust it to a potter who fires it to **bisque**. Not higher. Bisque can still be filed and refined to remarkable details.

Have the piece fired again and this time to hard porcelain. No **glazes**. You have now the replacement of the carved wooden Greek relief heads; it is hard like a stone and will serve forever.

Rub thin gold sheet over it, first with your fingers, then **only** with wooden tools, beginning at the middle level, working up and down, and annealing often.

When work with the wooden tool has reached its limits, use a polished steel burnisher to bring out the details, the porcelain model remaining in place. When the work is completed, remove the model and cut off all surplus metal along the outside. If **no** enamelling is intended, fill the back of the relief with epoxy (see Hints From A-Z), let it dry thoroughly, and flatten the filler. It is now ready to be set.

We never lose any precious material and that takes the fear away of contaminating the gold with solder. No rush—going slowly works faster. Only when you like what you have done, burnish very gently, and polish by hand. The *skirt* of the sketched figure in the illustration is made of a section of the shell.

I have enamelled over the entire surface of a relief, or over only parts of a relief, leaving parts of it gold metal. Counter enamel is used on gold only to give it strength. Silver needs counter enamel.

Firing softens the metal to a point where it may lose its shape and crispness. Here is the proven way to avoid that:

Make and fire a *pillow of reinforced ochre* (with thin iron wire), and rest the piece on it at each firing. It can be washed off. It is possible to lay cloisonné wires over such a relief.

The imprints of an ornament as simple as this sample might be sections of a rich, enamelled piece of jewelry, worn around the neck like a collar (it must be provided with rims to border the enamel on both sides).

Enamelled Figure in Relief
(Five and one-half-inches high—
a technical experiment)

It was curiosity which made me do it. Whenever I get set about a new challenge, I draw or model too naturalistic for my own liking, but by and by the idea behind it wins. I started modelling with plasticene on a piece of glass, the sketch having been glued under the glass. Next I cast a negative of this figure in plaster of Paris following all the steps already described, until I had the rock hard relief in porcelain and a thin copper-sheet copy of it. (0.3 millimeters thick).

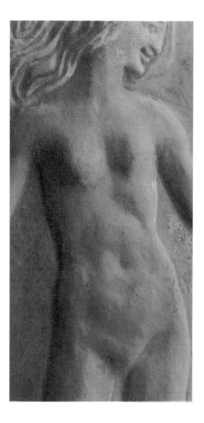 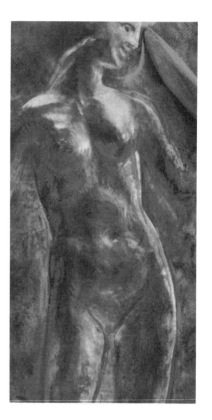

After acid cleaning and glass brushing, and to retain the relief high, I filled the back with ochre, sifted clear flux over the front, and fired the copper copy.

My intention was to add as many enamelling techniques as possible to this experimental piece.

After removing the ochre with water, the back received a heavy coat of counter enamel: spray glue, sift, spray, sift, and spray again. Then let dry.

While I wetpacked the front, I also placed cloisonné wires, filled them tightly, and put a drop of glue on each, since they covered parts of the very curvy surface. After drying thoroughly, I fired all at the same time.

The next step was to add contours and shading with oil-based painting enamel and grisaille—**enamel is patient, indeed!** My hope is that some enamellers will profit from this rather wild experiment and use it in good taste.

Chapter Six
Techniques for *Limoges* and *Champlevé*

Enamelling Limoges

Limoges, a town in France, was famous for this technique which gave it its name: enamel applied without cloisonné wires. It is wetpacked on fluxed

copper, with engraving under transparents, foil to increase the brilliance—everything is permitted.

My sample, set into the lid of a pewter box, shows just about all of that. Let us go through the different steps:

1. The design is applied to eighteen gauge copper.
2. Flux is fired over the engraved clean copper.
3. Silver foil and/or gold foil are glued into their places, and at the same time enamel, opaques, and transparents are wetpacked where they do not interfere with the foil. Fire.
4. Alternate wetpacking and firing until the desired result is achieved.
5. Gold-painted contours, maybe some goldgrains, are added.

The gold, which was mixed with thick oil of turpentine to a thick paste and thinned with oil of cloves, is applied generously. For the very high-lights and details in the shells, **grisaille-white** is painted, which is also oil-based like the gold, and dried carefully in the mouth of the open kiln. The volatile oils will burn out with a light smoke, the gold turns to a mustard color and the grisaille white looks yellow-brown at first, then changes to white. Corrections and sharpening of the lines can easily be made at this stage.

6. Insert the piece for a last firing into a barely red-hot kiln and remove it for a moment when you see a light shine on the grisaille. Try with a metal point to determine if gold and white have fused. If they can still be scratched off, put the piece back into the kiln.

7. The gold still looks matte, like cinnamon. By brushing it with a glass brush under running water, it shines mildly and beautifully. If you want a high polish, use a steel burnisher and a drop of soapy water.

For talented painters, this technique permits effects one would never dare with any other medium.

Champlevé—by Audrey B. Komrad

Preparing for the Etch

1. Use heavy copper, twelve or fourteen gauge.
2. Do all cutting and shaping of the copper first. Do not dome yet.
3. Anneal copper. Bring to a reddish glow in the kiln and plunge into cold water.
4. Pickle in warm Sparex #2 and rinse thoroughly in water.
5. Clean copper well. If you have a polishing machine, Lea Compound can be used. Rinse thoroughly in water.
6. Dry and rub surface gently with a brass brush till shiny. Rinse with water.
7. Design can be drawn freehand with Stabilo pencil or transferred from tracing paper with carbon paper, using a sharp pointed tool.
8. On those areas *not* to be etched, paint on acid resist such as Weber's Liquid Etching ground, any good Universal Etching ground, or asphaltum. Use a fine-pointed sable brush. Do not extend the design to the very edge of the metal. Paint the etching ground in a narrow border around the edge. This will give a neater design and protect the edge from chipping. When applying the acid resist, if the first applications too thin, go over the lines again. Dry and scratch some of the lines with a dull point, and enlarge some until you are pleased with the design. Very thin lines may be lost through undercutting. Acid resist lines should not be thinner than one-thirty-second-inch to one millimeter.
9. Allow to dry completely—overnight is best. Check the acid resist for complete coverage.
10. Melt bee's wax, paraffin, or candle wax. With an old brush, paint this on the back and edges of the copper. Do not go over the brush strokes of the design.

Etching Process

1. Using a pyrex dish (never metal), place two triangular glass or plastic rods in bottom.

2. Place the copper *upside down* on the rods so it is supported only on the border where the acid resist is painted.

3. Prepare the ferric chloride ($FeCl_3$) solution:
   Thirteen ounces $FeCl_3$ to thirty-two ounces water.
   It is best to use the ferric chloride in purified lumps. It keeps better than liquid or powder. Place the warm water in a plastic bucket. Weigh the lumps on a small scale. With rubber gloves, break up the lumps in the water with your fingers until they dissolve and go into solution. Remember, always add the $FeCl_3$ to the water, not the other way around.

4. Pour the solution into the pyrex dish till the level of the liquid is just up to the copper and not completely covering it. The action of the solution takes place on the surface of the liquid.

5. The solution must be stirred or the dish gently rocked from time to time, so bubbles will not be trapped on the copper surface and retard the etch. Use a wood stick to stir.

6. Occasionally check the etch. Using rubber gloves, remove the piece and place it immediately into a bowl of water. Otherwise, a green powder will form on the surface when $FeCl_3$ hits the air (it is *important* to note that if this green powder gets into a hot kiln, chlorine gas is formed and is dangerous to breathe in). The etch can be checked while holding it in a bowl of water. If you see a bright spot, scratch it with a dental tool or sharp instrument. This means an air bubble has been trapped there. If the etching ground has lifted off in some areas, rinse the piece gently in water, dry, and repair the lines. Dry completely before replacing it into the solution.

7. When the solution turns murky green, remove the copper with rubber gloves and place it in a bowl of water. Discard the old solution and add fresh. Replace the copper in the new solution as before.
   Never dispose of the old solution down the drain (most drains are copper). Neutralize it with a little ammonia and discard outside.

8. The etch should not go down more than half the thickness of the metal or it will be weakened. A good measure is to etch down to about the height of a cloisonné wire (0.8 millimeters to 1.0 millimeters). With the above formula, it will take approximately eight to ten hours to etch several two and one-half-inch or three-inch circles.

9. When the etch is completed, wash thoroughly in water, soak in an ammonia solution for about fifteen minutes, rub with a glass brush and rinse thoroughly in water.

10. To get multiple bites, after the first bite is completed, place the piece in water. Soak in ammonia solution for about fifteen minutes and rinse with water. Allow to air dry or pat gently with a soft towel so acid resist is not disturbed. Paint more acid resist on for the second bite. Return to the ferric chloride solution and continue etching. The first bite should be the deepest.

Some Additional Notes on Etching

1. Ferric chloride is not an acid by itself. Ferric chloride, in combination with copper, form hydrochloric acid. It does not have dangerous fumes like nitric acid and does not give an underbite like nitric.
2. Ferric chloride etches by gravity which is why the piece is etched upside down. (Nitric acid etches in all directions.) Also, ferric chloride etches only on copper, not on silver.
3. A larger container with more solution etches faster than a small container with the same amount of solution. The more exposed copper, the faster the solution is used up, and the weaker it becomes. The smaller the amount of exposed copper, the stronger the solution stays, and the faster it will etch.

Cleaning the Copper After the Etch

1. Etching ground can be removed with paint thinner or turpentine. The wax can be removed with very hot water by placing the piece into a small, old pan and heating gently on the stove.
2. Scrub the metal with a glass brush or toothbrush and hot water, detergent, and ammonia. Rinse well.
3. Place the piece in warm Sparex #2 for about fifteen minutes and wash and dry well.
4. Anneal and dome if desired. Also, drill any holes you need for jump rings, mountings, etc.
5. Rub gently with a brass brush till metal is shiny. Rinse in water.

Preparing for Enamelling

1. If the piece is not to be enamelled immediately, keep it wrapped in a paper towel so it is not exposed to air.
2. Paint Scalex on the front surface and dry.
3. Counter enamel the back with a color compatible with the colors you will use on the front. Fire.
4. Pickle in Sparex #2 and rinse in water.
5. Brass brush till metal is shiny and rinse.
6. Apply a *very* thin sifting of #1005 medium-fusing flux to the front. It is all right if the pink of the copper still shows through. Dry thoroughly and fire to orange peel.
7. You are now ready to wet inlay your colors.

Some Tips on Enamelling

1. Wet inlay *very* thinly or air will be trapped in the enamel and cause pits which will be seen after stoning.
2. Use colors which are compatible with the bare, untreated copper.
3. Use lots of gold and silver paillons. They are very effective in champlevé. When placing, use Klyr-Fire sparingly (mostly distilled water with a drop of Klyr-Fire only).

4. There will be fire scale up against the walls of the etched areas. This will destroy the edges of the silver foil. Use a small amount of opaque enamel up against these walls in areas where silver foil will go. This will not only protect your silver, but will enhance your design. Fire scale will not affect the gold foil.

5. If the etch is very deep, wet inlay two or three very thin layers of enamel beneath the foils to bring them closer to the surface and in order to catch and reflect the light.

6. Although the layers of enamel will be thin most of the way through, if you want a matte finish the enamel should be mounded higher than the surrounding untreated metal in the last one or two firings.

After the Enamelling is Completed

1. Use carborundum stone (coarse) or wet alundum stone (150 grit) until all the enamel (including the first layer of #1005 flux) is removed from the bare copper areas. Then use fine carborundum stone or alundum stone (220 grit) and continue stoning, also wet. Then use wet-and-dry emery papers (use wet), 220, 320, 400, and 600. Remember, each one you use removes some of the scratches from the one before.
   Don't rush through these steps. All scratches must be removed from both the enamelled surface and the bare copper surface.

2. Polish with Tripoli on a polishing machine. Wash with warm water, detergent, and ammonia.

3. Polish with red rouge on a polishing machine. Wash with warm water, detergent, and ammonia.

4. Rub with a soft cotton or flannel cloth.

5. The piece can now be gold-plated.

Chapter Seven
Cloisonné and Plique-à-Jour

Cloisons are minute flat wires which form a design in a net of cells which are filled with ground enamel colors and melted to a solid coat. Such a cloisonné will last without discoloration for centuries. This is a technique worthy for vessels and objects of great human importance.

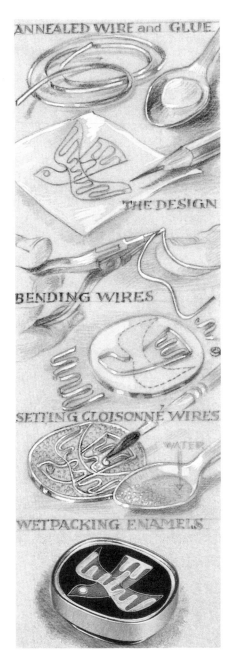

The metal carrier for large pieces will be silver or copper. The net of cloisons may be gold, 1000/1000 silver, or copper, which may be gold-plated. The norm is to fire a coat of clear flux to hold the wires on the front and counter enamel on the back. Only if the artifact is to be gold-plated should the wires be glued right on the clean copper. This way all metal has the direct contact necessary for electro-plating. In such a case, I let the net of cloisons dry and then sift the flux not only vertically on the plaques, but turn and move it to reach into all crevices.

It is quite amazing how many yards of cloisonné wire are used to cover a surface. To make it in my shop, I draw round copper or silver wire through a drawplate and roll it flat in a rolling mill to the desired height and thickness, a matter of trying and experience.

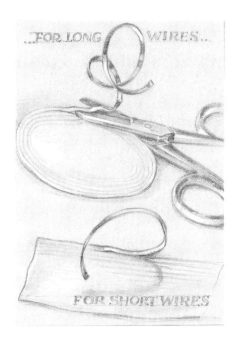

I prefer to cut gold wire in strips from thinly rolled sheet. Straight nail scissors do well. All wire must be annealed before bending it. I do feel free to bend my wires without forcing them with tweezers over the design by just looking, holding one end with the polished pliers, forming curves with a movement of wrist, fingertips, and pushing which produces lines and forms without efforts.

After dipping each wire into glue, I set it into its place. On curved surfaces, it must be fitted to the curve and held with some enamel and a drop of glue on top. In this manner we can fill large domed areas—even the entire outside of a cup—and fasten all wires permanently in one firing. **No** sudden jerks, please! The piece rests on a trivet and the firing fork. It is set into the hot kiln gently, the fork is removed, the door is closed, and there is only one thought in mind: To take it out at the right moment when the flux has melted and softened enough for the net of cloisons to adhere.

Still glowing hot, it is placed on top of the kiln and two hot spatulas are at hand to press with almost no effort over the whole surface. All wires are now permanently set.

Copper cloisons and bare copper produce a lot of oxidation after the first firing, so the piece needs to be immersed into an acid bath and, when clean, brushed with a **glass brush** under running water. A quick dip into diluted ammonia and into water, glass brush again, and start wetpacking the enamel. Fire when needed, layer upon layer, until all cells are filled higher than the wire net.

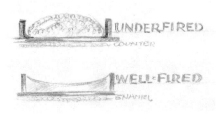

Larger areas of bare copper are painted with Scalex before each firing.

Stoning is a job we cannot get away without. As a last step I use wet-and-dry paper #360 until no more scratches are visible, neither on the enamel nor on the metal. Again water and glass brush, and a last filling of low spots then a drop of glue on top and the very last firing fast and hot—that's it.

There must be rims, or solid metal, wherever the enamel is exposed to pressure or easy damage.

To get a *three-dimensional effect* on an even surface:

Wetpack opaque enamel like a **relief**, the highest areas a bit higher than the top of the cloisons. These will be the highlights.

Dry well and fire just enough for the enamel to melt barely to an *orange peel* surface **not** losing the relief.

Next, with a gray transparent, wetpack the shades. Again fire but not yet to maturity. The relief must be retained. Only for the last firing fill the whole area tightly with a medium to soft flux, covering evenly the design of cloisonné wires. Dry and fire fast and high. What a surprising effect! It seems almost alive when it is taken out of the kiln.

I find the warmth of my hand to be ideal for rubbing the wax into the smooth enamel and to achieve a fine polish.

Cloisonné on and with gold seems technically like child's play: no oxidation, no counter enamelling, and no flux are needed. Colors are brilliant, and the danger to melt the gold is almost non-existent.

On silver we must remember that red, pink, and orange colors should be underlayed with the special flux for silver. The same holds for N-T gold as it contains silver. The melting point of silver is lower—watch out!

Small delicate gold and/or silver cloisonné pieces become true jewels when they are polished like a precious stone on a lapidary wheel. They should be treated and set like fine jewelry.

For religious pieces I suggest stopping when the enamelled surface is even, after being stoned and treated with #320 wet-and-dry emery paper; there are no more scratches, and it feels good. Wash with a glass brush under running water to remove every impurity, let the piece dry and then wax it with a good paste wax to revive the colors.

The design is fitted together from many details on drawing paper.

The balance of color is noted down with colored pencil.

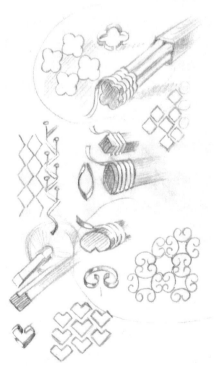

Repetitions of small cloisonné shapes to fill empty spaces in a design safely.

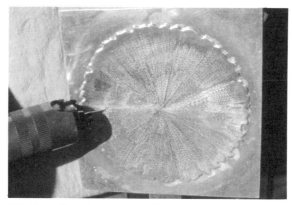

The fine-silver shape four-inches is set deep in the T&D method. To increase the reflection of transparent enamels, and for safe fusing of enamels on metal, the surface has been roughened.

The outer rim of the T&D serves as a stencil while bluish flux is sifted over the enamel-to-be.

Gold cloisons are bent...

...and set. A first coat of enamel holds them safely in place.

After several layers of enamel have been wetpacked with firings in between, the piece is *stoned*, finished,...

...and set. The T&D-made frame holds the words: "*Whoever receives such a child receives me*"

Plique-à-Jour

New York Collection of Museum of Modern Crafts

A flat piece of plique-à-jour is a relatively easy task if a few rules are kept: The height of the wires and the thickness of the sheetmetal should both be about 1.2 millimeters or 16 to 14 gauge; saw out the enamel-to-be and place it on **new mica**. Sew both with binding wire on wire-mesh.

This trivet of wire-mesh is very slightly domed, so that the three different materials are pressed together. Sawing out the openings reduces the risk. Fill the cells with light, freshly ground transparent enamel, packing it tightly with a drop of Klyr-Fire **on top**. The metal partitions are kept clean.

The hues should be very light and enamels chosen should have little tendency to crack. Blues are good, so are golds and grays—try them. Chartreuse is not good. The enamels are wetpacked with a slight hill in the middle of each cell; add a drop of glue, dry thoroughly, and fire high and fast. The molten enamel will now have concave indentations where hills were. Fill again with clean flux to keep the transparents light, fire, stone the surface evenly, polish all metal parts, and fire again until a pleasing clear surface results. Leave it concave. Or fill again, stone again, fire again.

Copper has to be acid cleaned between firings as long as oxidation builds up. *Fine silver* stays clean but expands and contracts, which can cause cracks with risky colors.

N-T gold (eighteen gauge thick) is ideal, but needs silver flux where red, pink, or orange colors touch the metal. With *pure gold* it is a *piece of cake*. Eighteen gauge thick seems rather wasteful, but for small excellent work, it is really sensible to use it.

This cup was made by my master student *Joanne Conant* and myself. Joanne's hands and my advice were the main tools. We both hope that our mutual achievement will be an inspiration, a catalyst to the many who might learn from it. Plique-à-jour on curved and vertical shapes, as in a cup, is rather challenging, but it is also a matter of understanding the why of what happens. A thin, spun or raised copper shape presents less problems than one with solder joints.

We had to have a **rim** on top and a foot for the cup to stand on, so this meant a wide enough rim to mount a nice foot after the cup was finished. Hard silver solder was used to add both without even the slightest opening. Both rims are to be sixteen gauge thick. The copper cup had to be as thin as it was safe to work over it in the cloisonné technique, with wires higher than normal: fourteen to sixteen gauge (1.2 to 1.3 millimeters). The width may be as wished.

Over the outside of the copper cup, one or two coats of hard clear flux was sifted and fired. No pores and no flaws, for acid might seep in and destroy the metal. The inside received counter enamel.

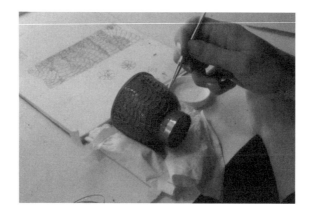

We were now ready to bend and set (glue on) the wires; each fitting the curve of the cup. A design with a great number of compact small cells makes it easy and logical. Where these wires touched a rim, I made it a point that they fitted into it. Joanne filed a small cleft for a safe hold. All cloisons had to touch, avoiding slim distances from each other, and be like a net around the cup.

All wires were set before the first firing and held with wetpacked enamel; a drop of glue on top formed a solid crust. Since this work proceeded in sections, the moisture was soaked out with tissue paper. First firing! When the cup was removed from the kiln, we had a hot spatula at hand and we had a second pair of hands to steady the glowing hot cup on the trivet and on top of a lazy susan, gently pressing the wires so that they sunk into the coating of flux without touching the metal cup.

All cells were filled like one would do with cloisonné but avoiding medium-dark transparents; clear, soft colors are better. The piece was stoned, finished, and checked to be sure there were no pores or openings in the enamel, then all metal was polished. A last firing; fast and hot, to an even glossy surface (if the enamel should droop a little inside the cells, see Chapter Thirty-three—it tells how to remedy it).

How did we get rid of the inside counter enamel? Heated bee's wax was thickly poured and painted over the *whole outside and the two rims*—**No** openings and no air bubbles left. The cup was placed into a strong plastic container with a lid, the insides of which were both coated with wax.

The waxed cup was placed into this plastic jar and hydrofluoric acid was poured into the cup. We covered it and left it alone—outside of the house, please! The acid eats the counter enamel away; now and then we helped the process with the brush of a feather.

When the counter enamel was gone, we washed the cup with water and ammonia and put it back into the cleaned container, then filled its inside with iron chloride, which attacks the copper, *not* the glassy enamel flux. It takes a while, and we retained only the flux, holding the net of cloisons and enamel.

The cup was warmed in water and brought to a temperature that would melt the wax and, therefore, let it swim on top. After cooling, the wax was removed, and there was our cup!

Our experiment in understanding the logic of this surprisingly attractive technique had worked. The thick coat of flux had kept the acid from the net of cloisons safely. The cloisons were higher than one would use them for cloisonné, because we wanted a solid cup. The very light hues let the light shine through, and the bare rims on top and around the bottom permitted nice metal work and further protection.

If one of you, our readers, wishes to follow our steps, please design a foot of more open work and maybe enhance it with precious stones.

These are **our** experiences. I see excellent work from Japan, England, and Cyprus; they may have differing enamels, although Joanne's and my method is foolproof (See Chapter Ten).

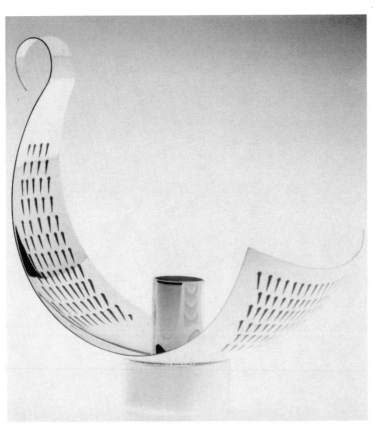

Candelabra designed and enamelled by Doctor Panicos E. Michaelides

Chapter Eight
Gold Granulation

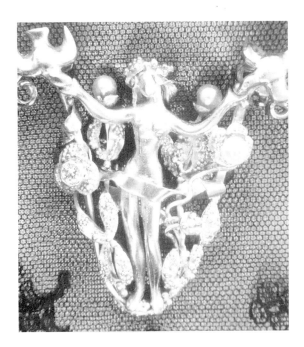

The process had to be quite simple. Ancient civilizations mastered it to such perfection that we find it almost beyond human abilities. They had *native gold* with only traces of copper and silver; they had organic glues and copper containing minerals (copper oxide); and they had charcoal and slaves. The Etruscans, the Egyptians, the Greek, and the Chinese knew it, and more of it than today's goldsmiths. What about the ancient tools: they had *no* saws, but scissors; no drawplates; next to no iron tools, but bronze; no mills, but knew how to hammer gold into very thin sheet.

The 1966 exhibit "Greek Gold" at the Brooklyn Museum and its excellent catalogue were an enormous help in understanding, thanks to Patricia Davidson.

With just as modest means I succeeded, not to the ancient mastership but well enough to share my results.

The tools I use are:

- A pair of scissors
- A charcoal block and powdered charcoal
- A crucible coated with graphite
- Gum tragacanth
- Liquid solder flux for precious metal
- Tweezers
- A sable brush #1
- A mouth blow torch for bottled gas
- A small spatula and a piece of matted glass two-inch-by-two-inch

There are two methods to produce gold grains or perfect minute gold spheres:

Method A

If a kiln going up to over 2000 degrees Fahrenheit is available, large amounts of granules can be made at the same time:

- Grind charcoal powder finely.
- From clean leftovers of N-T gold or twenty-two carat gold, cut tiny snips, as close as you can come to the same size.
- Spoon a layer of charcoal powder into the crucible and sprinkle the gold snips over it. They should not touch each other if possible; add another layer of charcoal, and yet another of gold snips. Repeat until the snips are all distributed.
- Avoid moving and shaking the filled crucible, or else the heavier gold will sink to the bottom and you get clots of gold but few single granules.
- Cover the filled crucible with a slab of *reinforced ochre*.
- Insert gently into the not yet hot kiln, and turn the heat on until it is at least 2200 degrees Fahrenheit.

I have tried to share a potter's kiln. It will work if the crucible is not moved around. Let it cool slowly and pour the content—gold and charcoal—into a glass with water. The gold falls to the bottom, the charcoal rises to the top—an easy manner to separate both.

- Sift the granules through graduated sieves and you separate the goldgrains into most delicate sizes.
- N-T gold remains clean. Twenty-two carat has a light oxidation (an acid bath helps) and fine gold (native gold) remains untarnished.
- The gold sheet to place the grains on and the grains must be of the same grade of gold.

Method B

The other method to produce gold spheres is slower but safe, if one invests just a few hours of patience:

- Take a new flat charcoal block (the kind goldsmiths use).
- Rub it over a brick or flat stone until it is smooth and even.
- Carve a deep line around its four sides—a ditch to catch any escaping spheres.
- Paint the whole surface with soldering flux (Fluoron).
- Use scissors to cut tiny snips from gold sheet metal and place them on the block without touching each other.
- Blow a small hot flame vertically on each snip and it will melt into a perfect sphere.

When the flat gold is prepared to receive the granules, polished and fitting the design:

Mix (fresh each time) on a matted glass slab with a spatula:

- a drop of gum tragacanth soaked with liquid solder flux or water
- a minimal amount of copper oxide
- and, as thinner, again Fluoron
  (solder flux for precious metal).

This thinned mixture holds the grains in place. The copper oxide helps the welding process.

Either dip granules into this mix and put them into place with watchmaker's tweezers, or place them with the tip of a brush, one by one, on an area moistened with copper oxide mix. If the grains are very small, place as many as reasonable, pushing them into the planned ornament on a drop of the copper oxide mix.

Leave alone and let dry thoroughly. If I set the grains in the evening, I apply the flame the next morning.

Both flat or curved gold and the grains must be heated to the **same intense heat**, which shows by the same color of **glowing up to lemon-yellow**. It takes nerves at the beginning, but you *cannot* lose or contaminate the gold. You *can* lose the time invested in your work.

Suddenly the heat is so high that a liquid flush seems to run over the piece. That is the moment when grains and metal become one. Try with a tool whether the grains are on; some may not be, so replace them and go through the same process again.

Such a piece of granulated gold can be enamelled or can be bent slightly, it **is one**, indeed, and may be set and be integrated into any design.

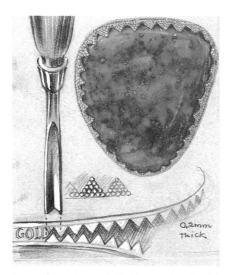

A wood carving tool divides a strip of gold into two lengths for a bezel.

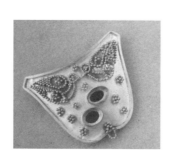

Chapter Nine
Grisaille

My work with grisaille is spread over so many years that I had to make a new sample to revive my experiences and give the best information possible. The drawing of an iris seemed right, because figures can be a bit problematic for enamellers who are less experienced with the human image.

As metal I strongly suggest using copper or fine gold for small and precious pieces (not N-T gold, which contains silver). The difference is few dollars and the safety of using the best material prevents problems. Silver might cause cracks in the grisaille design, which cannot be repaired.

No flux, just immaculately clean enamel sifted over the surface. If possible sift and fire the front and the back of the plaque at the same time. If it cannot be done, apply a coat over the front first.

The front without counter enamel will slightly dome by itself. Then take care of the back. The front receives one or two coats of thinly sifted enamel. For the iris sample I did not bother to go through the proper transferring of the design, but painted right from the drawing. If it is not quite what one wants, it can easily be wiped off and be done over. The white is #497 from Schauer, available in USA. Thompson-Enamel has an extremely fine ground white which I have seen successfully used in large grisailles. I do mix the white with a minute drop of thick-oil-of-turpentine to give it substance, and I use lavender oil, which evaporates as fast as a thinner. As you see on my photograph I painted the highlights too heavily. A veil-like quality should remain, although too thin painting might disappear in the fire. While I usually do only one coat, especially when I work on very small pieces, I had to add a second coat over the iris. Drying the piece extremely well in the mouth of the open kiln is important. The small amount of thick oil changes the work into a real ugly dark brown, but after a while the oil burns off and the white reappears. That means you may fire, watching carefully; try on the hot piece if the white has fused. You can do that on some unobtrusive spot with a metal point. The painted surface will stay matte but if you want it glossy and protected, sift a very thin veil of glass clear flux over it, the softest flux you can get. Fire not quite to maturity and add a second coat which is fired to an even shine.

Safe background colors are transparent blues. Olive green, gray, lavender, and, of course, opaque black will do well. I used a hard orange transparent in several coats, stoned to perfect evenness in between, fired, and got a deep brown which worked well on copper. My suggestion is to make samples, and experiment with them to find out the best results.

If someone had the intention to produce a large plaque or plate in grisaille rich with figures, one would automatically think of seventeenth century grisailles depicting a super-muscular Hercules. In my sample I preferred the charm of the Three Graces as a theme for the instruction I am giving here.

Let me explain how to proceed safely and relaxed in producing such an enamel: Bare of all responsibility, I begin with freely sketching on tracing paper. Slowly the composition emerges. When turned over, the tracing paper shows disproportions and mistakes, which we can correct on the front. Soon the three girls begin to smile back.

Each of the vertical lines on my sketch connect the center of the neck with the weight-carrying foot which means the figure will not tip over.

The next overlayed tracing paper is to be strong, very transparent, and must remain flat when used with watercolor. I go over the design again and, with tempera white, the highlights are set and the pleasing roundness develops. But I still have a regular drawing, dark on white. However, the pre-work for grisaille must be *white on a dark* background.

Here is a safe method: Place the drawing on very dark paper. The pencil lines remain barely visible. Cover both with a piece of clean glass and fasten all three layers (dark paper, drawing, and glass) on a drawing board.

Now proceed with white artist's oil paint, thinned with painting medium, translating the design onto the glass slab. We do not paint shadows, we paint the different shades of light. What you do not like is easily wiped off. Dark lines are scratched through the white paint with a plastic point. All searching and thinking is done now, without any concern of ruining a good enamel-to-be.

Artist's white oil paint is used over dark background.

There comes a moment when on this side of the glass we can do no more. Construct a frame-like contraption on which to rest the glass safely, separate the three layers, and turn only the glass over. You have now a dry clean side to continue and apply the last fine details and finishing touches on your model.

You have now the experience *and* a perfect model.

Model for the final execution in grisaille.

After the oil colors are completely dry, place a thin tracing paper over it, and mark the few main points of the composition on the tracing paper, which are rubbed on the backside with white chalk. If the chalked side of the tracing paper is laid over the cleanly enamelled plaque, trace the guiding points with a sharp pencil. You can now copy your model on the plaque.

Chapter Ten
Two Chalices with Cloisonné All Over and Lined with Gold-plated Inner Cups

A. Family Cup

(owned by Hans Zeitner)

Who has not dreamt of that nobly shaped chalice, enamelled all over with immaculate transparents, maybe just one fine gold line winding around its outside—so elegantly understated, so utterly simple. That is **poetry**. It would neither work nor last. A chalice has to withstand very hard use, and maybe even abuse. It must be carefully planned. That is why I have made this cup as a teaching example. We use this cup at festive occasions, when everybody takes a sip from it. A nice translation of the Jewish *Kiddush* cup into every family's life.

The design is as simple as can be: a very large number of small shapes, easy to fit to the curved surface. I have been thinking of a tree with roots, a trunk, and a blossoming crown in which creatures live. Of course, one could have that winding line, but it must be broken up into small hairpin-like shapes, all curved to fit safely to the body of the cup. But even then, it would be wise to cover the whole surface with a net of fine cloisonné shapes touching each other. The Orientals have used this concept for hundreds of years and with good reason.

Anneal the wires well, so they do not stretch during firing. Finally, when the many parts of the cup are to be assembled, it is important that there will never be any pressure on the enamelled parts. A metal rim or bezel, etc., will take care of this problem. If hit, only one or two cells will be damaged, and the net of wires would take the impact. Such small defects can be repaired, reshaped, fired, gold-plated, and put together again. Our *dream cup* would have cracked all over and be a complete loss.

Counter enamel works fine for two or three firings. However, it would be a miracle if it remained perfect in the many firings and stonings of a chalice—too much of a risk.

Religious cups must be gold inside (gold plating the inside will do the job). Wine may leave spots on enamel, and one should not drink from enamel if it is not lead free. Pure gold needs no counter enamel, and it holds enamel because it expands similar to it.

The better the material, the easier the work. N-T gold is beautiful to work with. The cloisonné wires remain clean, and transparents are excellent over it except for reds, pink, oranges, and some purples. These transparents should be fired over a pre-fired coat of flux for silver. The same holds true for pure silver, but silver changes size in the kiln since it expands. I use only medium to soft enamels with fine silver (that means melting at low to medium heat).

My answer to all these problems is the lining cup, which is inserted into the outer enamelled cup. I will now demonstrate it with photography and pen. By the way, if you understand this particular construction, you can dream up almost anything safely—whole sculptures if you wish. I have avoided complicated skills, like raising metal, and have kept to a very few essential ones: clean soldering, fitting, and thinking.

The viewer sees only the very skin of a piece. He has no idea how much thought and skill is below its appearance—fun, too.

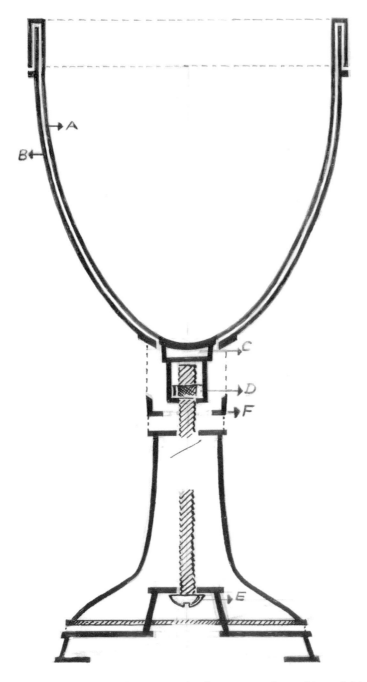

A careful construction drawing is the first step in the making of this cup. Once this is done and clear in our head, we can proceed part by part. Rims, etc., are provided for all spaces to be enamelled. This crosscut shows how I engineered the whole cup together.

A. The **inner cup**, to be polished and gold-plated, holds the **nut housing**.
B. The **outer cup** is to be enamelled.
C. **Space** between **cup** and **bolt**, to avoid the bolt touching the bottom of the cup.
D. The **steel nut** is soldered into the bottom of the **housing**.
E. The **bolt** is the backbone of the cup and holds all parts together.
F. **Ring** to cover joints.

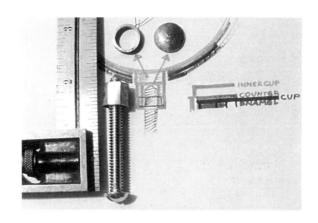

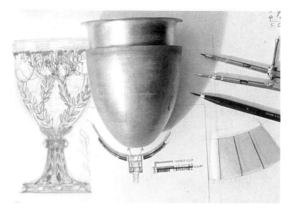

I like to snap in a small gold-plated cover over the nut, which can be easily removed if disassembling is needed.

Here we have the *outer cup*, which will be enamelled, and the lining cup, which will be polished and gold-plated.

The outer cup received a rim close to the top and a disk at the bottom. The enamel is safe between these two. The cup is ready for a coat of flux outside, and counter enamel inside. Do not enamel above the rim.

The lining cup receives the rim to be visible above the enamel. It is soldered after very carefully checking the exact width needed to insert the unenamelled rim of the enamelled cup.

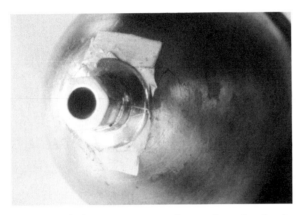

To find the exact center, the nut housing is placed over a piece of paper, on which the marks are made.

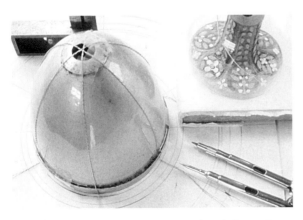

We can now concentrate on the cloisonné enamel. To divide it into six equal sections, the cup is centered over circles drawn on paper and the six partitions are marked.

After placing and checking the cup on the vertical, I put six pieces of thread over the center hole with plastic tape. With a Stabilo pencil I marked lines along the threads and...

...continued drawing the structure for the design of cloisons. I used very *simple shapes*, glued them to the surface with Klyr-Fire, section by section and filled them right away with enamel—all the way around.

The water is soaked out of the enamel with a tissue paper, and then a drop of Klyr-Fire is placed on top of each cell.

The flux underneath permits transparent enamels side by side with opaque enamels.

To be able to turn the cup without touching the enamel, I screwed and wired a small trivet as a stop for the rim, and a larger one touching, **but with some leeway**, for the bottom of the cup, both attached to strong wire mesh.

When faced with the question: How to invent a contraption for a special purpose? It amuses me that my experience always tells me: Everything is right there—just open your eyes.

After all cloisons were set, filled, and held by Klyr-Fire, I thought that I was ready to fire. But let me confess, my kiln ceiling was not high enough. The cup standing upside down on the wire mesh touched the ceiling of the kiln. I phoned a friend who lived thirty curvy miles away on a hilltop and told her, "Don't ask questions, just turn your kiln on high—I'll be there in forty-five minutes!" I placed the unfired cup into something like a safe box by my side on the floor of my car.

The cup and I arrived safely. The kiln was hot, and the cup did not lose a grain of enamel—it came out perfect. So much for Klyr-Fire! The following firings were done at the friend's kiln. After stoning all wires out, I fired the cup one last time, quick and hot for good color, again in the upside down position. But the enamel in each cell had slid down just enough to be impossible. There was only one answer: Fire it standing on its round bottom. But how?

I put one of those small metal trivets into the cup and stitched it tightly with iron wire to the wire mesh. It stood. This might sound a bit unprofessional to you, but it was the only way to solve the problem with what was at hand at the moment. If I had to make fifty cups, I would improve my inventions.

Keeping my eyes on the cup standing in the hot kiln, I watched for the moment when the enamel would slide back. It did, and at that moment, I took the cup out. I bathed it in Sparex, stoned lightly to get the even matte surface, waxed it, polished, gold-plated, and it was ready for the final assembling.

And now the foot; it is handmade, not spun, of two parts that are soldered with hard silver solder and shaped over a stake. It could have been raised, but I have aimed this whole project towards those enamellers who do not know too much about metalwork, but wish to widen their abilities.

Over the same stake I raised a second domed shape—cut it out and tied it over the first one with iron wires and soldered it to its base.

The right part of the picture shows the nut housing with the steel nut already in it, and the bottom rim on which the cup will stand. Solder is placed on the inside, where it cannot harm the enamel.

As you can see, the verticals do not reach all the way up the foot. I had to add six strips of copper by hard soldering. Where these six strips meet the ornament, the seams will show. I knew it. It could not be avoided. You will see the answer. I drilled six small holes at the problematic seams.

The wires were glued with Klyr-Fire right on to the copper. There was no flux underneath because all the enamel on the foot is opaque. However, the inside received a generous sifting of flux, held in place with the sprayed-on glue.

Again I filled all cells at the same time, soaked the water out, and put that drop of Klyr-Fire on top of each cell. I filled the cloisons just enough to hold the wires in place and avoid oxidation, and fired.

There were more firings, and with them the danger of the piece warping just enough out of shape so as not to fit anymore. Do remember this little trick: Form a substantial pillow of old iron binding wire and stuff it with moist ochre.

A piece of wire should stick out of the middle as a handle. The ochre-wire pillow was inserted into the hollow of the foot. It was dried well before, firing it separately in a hot kiln. It remains a bit crumbly, but holds well enough when put into the foot before each future firing with a bit of wet ochre to secure it. To soak all moisture out, I inserted the foot upside down into a hole, which in this case was a plastic tape container padded with paper towel.

The foot rests safely while the enamel is applied. A trivet on a clean surface props up the foot in a workable position while not touching the enamel—even a spool with iron wire serves this purpose.

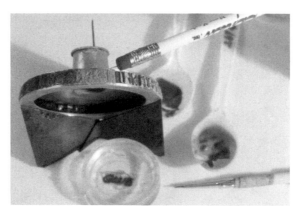

All is ready for the final firing: The last layer of enamel is packed higher than the cloisons, so that there will not be any low spots after stoning.

Stone and then a fine paste wax rubbed over the matte enamel. Polish with a soft cloth and this section is finished.

To enamel the base is about the same as the other parts. See to it that the letters touch the rims, or you might get cracks. It is most important that you apply a good layer of enamel on the inside, especially at the bottom rim!

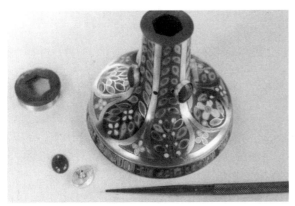

Hiding the six holes in the foot (remember, this is the way the old masters of the twelfth century did it, too!).

The copper ring at the right covers the connection of cup and foot.

Six corals are set into the curved bezels, underlayed with soft leather, which makes up for the curvature. The bezels are held to the foot by six strong round wires, with cut thread at the end. Small fitting nuts are screwed tightly at the inside.

Here is our cup! The line of poetry on the foot reads in German: *Trinkt ihr Augen, was die Wimper hält, von dem gold'nen Überfluss der Welt.*

(English: Drink my eyes what your lids can hold of the golden abundance of the world.)

B. The Cup of '88

(owned by Hans Zeitner)

A different approach:

The upper part of the cup speaks of hope, trust, healing, and healthy thinking. Again, I have found it best to express this with figures from the Bible, to say what is really almost impossible to address universally. You see Saint Michael and, underneath him on the foot, the atom bomb and some of its victims. Also, two of the symbols which seem to run the world: the dollar sign and the atom. On the other side of the cup is a human couple with their child—all is right and full of life.

On the foot sits that evil creature, destruction itself, holding mankind in chains like an animal of burden; the dollar sign above the whole unpleasant and too true scene; and the victims, woman and child, to his left.

In the twelfth century, such drawings would have been the picture-language that people understood. A man of great insight once said to me, "The artisan's work fills its purpose the moment it is made. True art appears to be quite unnecessary when it is first created and without bearing influence on the day's events, but what art has to give, grows; it is irreplaceable, be it poetry, philosophy, music, or the visual arts. It is mankind's best!" I hate to add—art is witness to mankind's worst as well.

Hold a small art object of the past in your hands, and almost-forgotten cultures with their ways of social thought and values come to life, especially if the observer knows history.

I hope to invoke such reflections when the reader carefully looks at this cup which, in my very late years, I felt I had to make. It was not made for anyone in particular. It began to take shape while I was sketching half-consciously, out of deep concerns we all shared at the time. Some of these concerns, thank Heaven, have almost become history! However, this cup will last and hold its message as long as it is not destroyed by violence or stupidity.

Since I have used ivory on the foot, I wanted to use the same color around the top. Incorporated into the design are lettering and symbols. The cup has two main fronts: One is Saint Michael fighting the fiery dragon (our present day atom bombs). The other side's theme is man, his woman, and child—the promised paradise—or is it the lost one? The setting of all wires around the cup as well as the enamelled text around the upper rim were done before the first firing, over a coat of clear flux. The Latin text reads:

Et ne nos induca in tentationem, se libera nos a malo.
In English: And lead us not into temptation, but deliver us from evil.

Let us look at a few technical details which were missing in the previous article, the Family Cup.

The gold plating of the enamelled part of the inner cup must be done professionally and with a fresh plating solution. This will help to avoid cracking. I do not like to use a coat of nickel plating first. It adds a raised surface over the enamel and looks cheap.

Let me close with a word by Ingmar Bergman: "...it is my opinion that art lost its creative urge the moment it was separated from worship....creative unity and humble anonymity are forgotten....the smallest cuts and moral pains of the ego are examined under the microscope as if they were of eternal importance."

Chapter Eleven
A Study of the Construction of Medieval Artifacts

Introduction

I do not say this is how the seven artifacts have been made, because I could not hold them in my hands, but it is how we, today, could make them. How much we can learn from intensely looking at them!

It is heartbreaking to think of all the beauty which has been vandalized and stolen from Byzantium such as the gold melted down just for the *material* value and perhaps for easier transportation of the booty. During those dark ages the Christian religion had slowly, slowly grown roots in Europe, Ireland, the south of Germany, along the Rhine, and in what is now the French south. Monasteries were founded, churches built, and the need for sacred vessels and objects grew.

Small Byzantine gold altars had come to the west in those chaotic days. But what once was "West Rome" was poor and there was not enough gold except for gilding objects of copper. The skills of making and designing sacred vessels and artifacts had to develop slowly. It was the monasteries which saved what was left from the dying culture of Rome. There were men living in them who were able to create something very new—quite primitive at the beginning, but with an aura of great dignity and with an inner power of devotion and belief. We call it **romanesque** today.

All monasteries were connected by the Latin language and there must have been a remarkable intellectual exchange. The monasteries were also the treasure houses of the nobility who had no moral problems to use and misuse them. The monk-artisans were capable enough to engrave and strike coins with bronze and iron punches, and with this "know-how" they could also produce relief heads of saints to become part of enamelled reliquaries. We see the whole group of artists and the patrons of their art unfolding.

This will help you, my readers, to look with greater understanding at what follows in this chapter and which, I hope, will inspire you to works of your own art.

The men of the ninth to the fourteenth centuries were no miracle workers, but were very logical masters of their special skills: designers, engravers, sculptors in metal, goldsmiths, woodworkers, and casters combined their efforts to create pieces which make the visitors of great museums of the world exclaim, "Nobody can do this today!"

How did they make it? How did they put it together?

11.1 House Reliquary

The six enamels in Champlevé technique are fastened in the simplest manner on to a wooden boxlike core which has four solid wood cubes as feet. If a relic was placed inside, it must have been done while either part of the roof or one side was still open, or such a house reliquary has a door, an opening on one of the gabled sides.

The background is "God's Own Heaven," a traditional design found in large mosaics like this detail from the ceiling of the Empress Theodora's Mausoleum in Ravenna. We find these motifs on medieval bible covers, crosses, and uncountable religious artifacts.

To engrave the figures was comparably easy, but when it came to the faces of saints and sinners, not all men working with metal and enamel were capable designers. Also, the output of similar pieces was quite high and everything had to be done by hand. Those small metal heads which could be made with the strong blow of a hammer must have been a most welcome solution.

11.2 Thirteenth Century Ciborium, Louvre, Paris

This is a receptacle for the chalice when it is not needed to celebrate mass. The basic metal is copper which was mercury-gilt after all enamelling had been done. The background is again the traditional dark blue with its stars.

The making and mounting of the Ciborium is clearly shown by the design. Please study carefully the heavy hinges on one side holding a door and a lock.

Enamellers today would not engrave the deep spaces for the enamel. They would etch them deep and use an acid which keeps a clean line: *iron chloride* (see Chapter Six, "Champlevé"). Mercury gilding (see Chapter Thirty-three, "Hints from A-Z") is so dangerous that it is no longer done commercially. But the fine-gold shine and beauty of it cannot easily be achieved by electro-plating.

11.3 House Reliquary

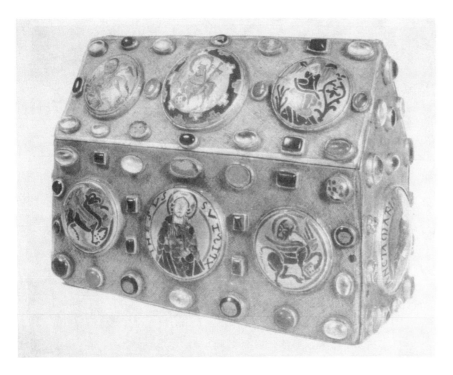

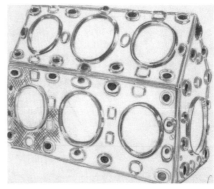

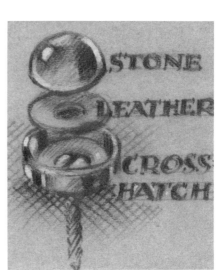

The fourteen enamelled medallions are set separately. The six thick copper plaques are not enamelled but are enlivened by a cross hatch of engraved lines and bezels for stones and enamels. After being gilt the effect is extremely precious with such simple means.

How could one proceed to make a similar "box" today?

a) First, one would make the fourteen medallions, finished to perfection and ready to be set like cabochon stones.
b) The six copper panels receive a surface treatment. In the case of this reliquary, it is a cross-line engraving.
c) Bezels to hold the enamels and the stones are soldered on each, and holes for screws are drilled where the red dots appear inside these bezels.
d) After gold-plating, the enamels are set and the six plaques are screwed to the wooden core.
e) To avoid any problem in setting the stones, the screws are covered with leather. This also secures a good fitting.
f) Set the stones. (The relic probably rested on and was wrapped in fine fabric, and was inserted before final mounting.)

Such treasures were shockproof and desirable values to the church in times of turmoil to pay with—or to become loot.

As far as a shock-proof investment goes, they still are.

11.4 A Small Portable Folding Altar

It folds together like a book. This is not an exact description of the shown altar. I hope to inspire goldsmithing enamellers and enamelling metal smiths, in case their task is to create a precious receptacle for an honored object.

Gold-plated altars like this were carried into battle and taken on long voyages. They served as focus points for collecting all the energy, trust, and faith a man or woman could come up with. They had probably gone through many hands and many perils and the owners knew themselves to be protected by its power. When we ask ourselves sincerely if such meditation helped, the answer is YES!

It lifted the spirit and made the heart brave—or very patient for accepting the will beyond one's own.

Translate all this into an artifact, made today. It need not be part of any special religion, but it must be a symbol, it must speak that language of humanity that everybody understands. There is a need for pieces of this kind, and they must not be too complicated, not too precious, and not too perfect—done with the naivete of a child's prayer and its concentration.

The metal covering on this old piece is almost patched together and held with rivets, and the stones on the closed outside are my way to mount all parts safely. When the altar is closed none of the inside relief must touch.

I would cut the figures negatively in plaster of Paris, make porcelain imprints, and work the metal over these; then enamel and counter enamel each. For the cross, the wings of the angel's halos and the architecture on the right wing, I suggest the T&D technique. The frames should not be enamelled, but be part of the wooden core, and the gold-plated metal should be intelligently mounted in combination with all other parts.

The crosscut shows the basic wooden shape and how the enamelled relief figures and the arches are mounted.

11.5 The Great Altar of Nikolaus from Verdun Twelfth Century, Cloister Neuburg, near Vienna, Austria

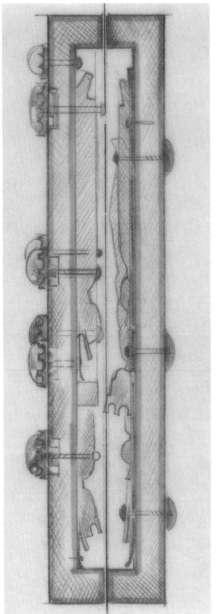

Do imagine a gold-plated, enamelled wall over 5 meters in width and 1.08 meters high (about three-and-a-half-feet high). It consists of hundreds of single enamels rich in figures, wonderful lettering, and ornaments built up in six levels, plus frame, and all in perfect harmony and order.

How could men plan and execute such a masterpiece, build their workshops and kilns, and melt and grind their colors with the chemical know-how needed for such an enterprise? Their talent and the work of their hands and minds still speak their strong language after 800 years.

They travelled as a large company of metalsmiths, engravers, designers, and chemists to produce the enamels; and travelling across Europe with them were the wood workers, gilders, and those for the hard physical tasks and services. They needed everything: living quarters, food—and time.

Those men and their patrons had completely different values but very positive ones! Their work was indeed done for the glory of God. Put yourself, for a moment, into the place of these artisans (I am quite certain they did not consider themselves to be **artists**). What a joy they must have felt when their work was near completion, step by step. I marvel about the genius of the man Nikolaus von Verdun, who could conceive and organize all this.

The first executed plan had not been for a triptych but for a pulpit. In the year 1130, a fire destroyed the town of Neuburg and the monastery. The chronicler writes that the enamels could only be saved by dousing them with wine. After the fire, in 1131, the enamels became the main part of an altar. One fact might have helped to preserve the enamels: Their melting point was much higher than the temperature of the fire. Too bad that nails were used to hammer the parts into place—that did a lot of damage.

An interesting surprise was that on the back of one of the enamelled plaques is an engraved design, done masterfully, perhaps by Nikolaus von Verdun himself, which shows us the very start of the work. The composition has certainly sprung from the minds of the most knowledgeable members of the order, for a deep meaning connects all fifty-one large plaques.

I am most grateful to the priest who let me study the altar, sketch, and photograph and indeed understand its construction. We see it today, well-lighted with electricity, but in ages past the people stood before it with candles, and reading the messages each plaque held in such mystic surroundings—only sometimes the colors would flash up like precious stones.

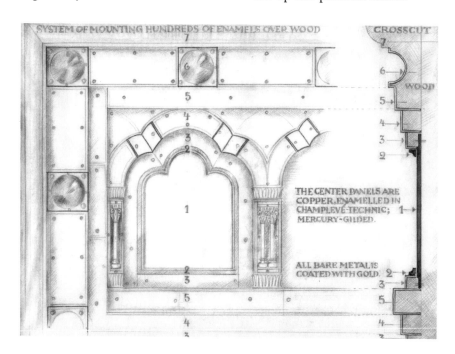

Let me now explain all that I learned about the construction. Maybe it will inspire a group of *tomorrow* to create a piece which holds the problems and answers of our troubled century, as well as its ingenious insights into the microcosm and eternal space, glorifying creation, not destruction.

These figures remained bare metal with deeply engraved outlines, which were filled with dark blue enamel. All backgrounds are opaque enamels in a limited number of colors: bluish-white, medium blue, light blue, and dark blue; green, a reddish-brown, and sometimes a rough mix of colors, which give the impression of stone or granite. The blues are often not separated by metal line, but wetpacked side by side. Today we would have to etch the sunken areas. The strips which surround the lettering and the plaques are champlevé plus cloisonné, ornamented like Byzantine gold cloisonné. A tradition still living, but done with the modest means of western Europe in the early Middle Ages.

How would such a task be done today? After the leading idea and content are clear and the size of the finished artifact decided upon, I would construct a small model, exact in proportion (using architect's board, no design yet). Next a ratio of one-to-one model of one section gives all the different shapes and sizes which will be repeated over and over again. This model shows where to overlap the metal, where to provide for screws, etc.

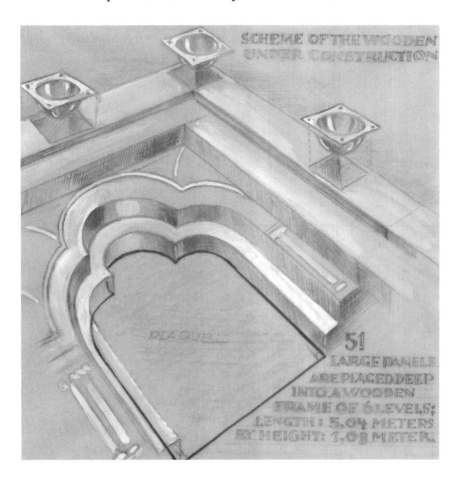

The next step is to cut the exact patterns of all the shapes to be used over and over again from x-ray film. Then saw these shapes from copper: eighteen gauge if it is to be cloisonné, twelve to fourteen gauge for champlevé. The thickness is to provide enough material for etching, probably in several depths. And **now** we concentrate on the designs. After all copper shapes have been counter enamelled, (do not forget to paint Scalex on the fronts-to-be). Chapter Six provides the information about cloisonné and etching champlevé.

Meanwhile the woodworker will have built the backing, and the enamelling can proceed piece by piece. To avoid irregularities, I suggest working on three or four enamels at the same time—those which are to be mounted side by side. Of course, we have reliable color samples at hand, but anybody who gets himself involved in such a project would have that anyway.

11.6 Twelfth Century Reliquary of Henry II, Paris Louvre

This was made in Hildesheim, Germany, for Henry II. The material is copper, and mercury gilt. It stands about thirteen inches tall. As I try to explain a **possible method** of construction of such an artifact, I do hope that it will be an inspiration for a gift of honor or a container for something very precious and dear.

Nobody quarrelled in those old days about what was art and what was only handcraft. Everybody was an artisan—some could draw, some were better in other trades, and all worked together.

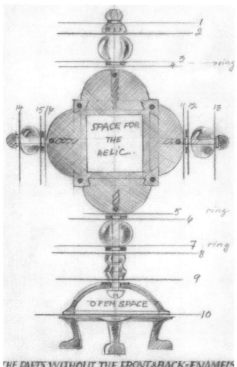

This illustration shows that this object consists of sixteen different parts, and very heavy copper was used—twelve to fourteen gauge thick.

What is seen as black would be covered with asphaltum to prevent etching. Front and back should be slightly domed for stability and for better access when stoning. The wide metal rims will hold the screws.

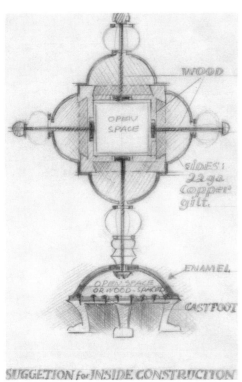

SUGGETION for INSIDE CONSTRUCTION

This illustration shows the wooden core with the open space in the center. The foot may be mounted over wood. The width of the wooden spacer is covered with twenty-two gauge gold-plated copper shaped over the wooden core, and held by gold-plated brass screws. The heads of these screws are filed to be a cross.

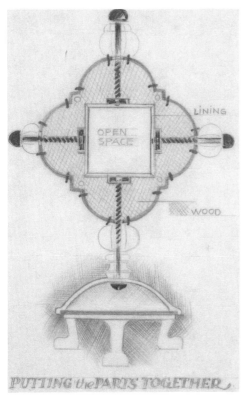

PUTTING the PARTS TOGETHER

The open space in the center maybe a door or may be covered with glass or an enamel. The crosscut explains how the parts fit, hold and become a solid piece.

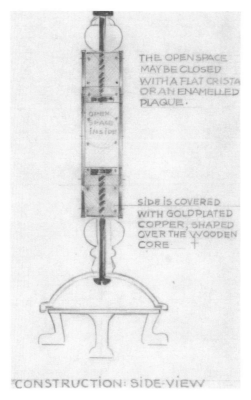

THE OPEN SPACE
MAY BE CLOSED
WITH A FLAT CRISTA
OR AN ENAMELLED
PLAQUE.

OPEN
SPACE
INSIDE

SIDE IS COVERED
WITH GOLDPLATED
COPPER, SHAPED
OVER THE WOODEN
CORE +

CONSTRUCTION: SIDE-VIEW

This is a side view crosscut.

The bolts have a thread cut where such is needed. If they traverse clear beads, the brass bolts should be polished. When assembling this piece, a neat lining covers the inside.

These sketches should be self-explanatory. The lining which hides the nuts and the inside wood might be either gold-plated copper, twenty gauge silver, leather, or velvet.

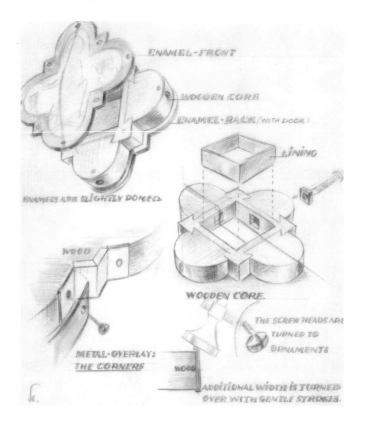

ENAMEL-FRONT

WOODEN CORE

ENAMEL-BACK (WITH DOOR)

LINING

ENAMELS ARE SLIGHTLY DOMED.

WOOD

WOODEN CORE

THE SCREW HEADS ARE
TURNED TO
ORNAMENTS

METAL-OVERLAY:
THE CORNERS

WOOD

ADDITIONAL WIDTH IS TURNED
OVER WITH GENTLE STROKES.

11.7 Ciborium

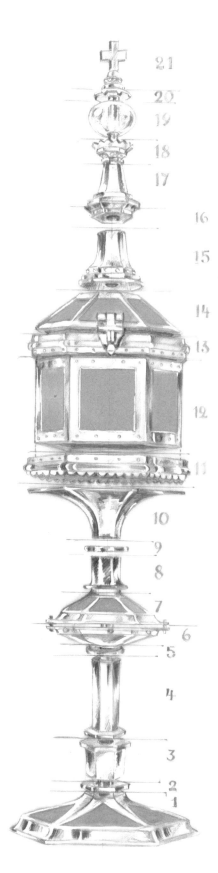

This Ciborium from the twelfth century, now in the Pierpont-Morgan Library, New York City, *is a chalice-shaped receptacle for the holy bread.* Yes, let us be impressed, deeply impressed—but not too much and not to the point where the goldsmith and the enameller give up. When I took hours at the Pierpont-Morgan Library to study this piece, to sketch it, to look at it from all angles and, indeed, made the watchman quite nervous, it was like a great lesson given to me by our colleagues from the twelfth century. And that is exactly what I wish to pass on to you.

However let me make the point that this is how we, today, might handle such a task, respectively a similar project.

The drawing shows twenty-one numbered spaces.

Number one is the foot. The detail drawing shows the patterns for the foot and the nodus, still flat, and the spaces where enamels are to be.

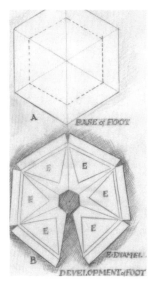
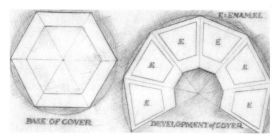

Number two is a thick ring-like hectagonal, an in-between step to number three, which is slightly wider than the top of the foot and number three, and helps to compensate a minute discrepancy between the two.

Numbers three, four, five, and six are work for the metal smith and are self-explaining. I suggest providing all four with a wooden core.

Number seven corresponds with the foot and its elevation can be seen on the detail drawing.

Numbers eight, nine, and ten are again the metal smith's challenges, also over a wooden core.

Number eleven is the base of the inner open space.

Number twelve must fit inside the rim of number eleven and the *wooden floor.* This vertical hectagonal wall holds six enamelled plaques, which are mounted on the wooden wall, and covered around their six sides with long strips of metal windows, folded around the hectagonal body of wood and twelve roundheaded rivets or nails, fabricated in the metal shop, to secure a tight fit.

Number thirteen is all metal. It covers the open inside space and must be of a strong enough construction to safely hold hinges and part of the lock. Here, between numbers twelve and thirteen, is the access to the inner chamber.

Number fourteen's wooden core inside provides for the nut of the upper bolt and its metal and enamel outside corresponds again to the foot and the nodus. See detail drawing.

Numbers fifteen, sixteen, seventeen, and eighteen are metal worked over wood.

Number nineteen is a large bead of semi-precious stone, and since this one is transparent, the part of the bolt visible through the bead, is gold-plated and well-polished. As an alternative—providing the drilled hole in the bead permits it—a fitting piece of tubing may line the threaded bolt.

Numbers twenty, and twenty-one, a domed metal ring, heavy enough to be flat on top, connects the bead and the upper bolt, which has a cross as a top.

The Crosscut is self-explaining.

Depending on the size of the object to be made, I suggest using copper sheet sixteen gauge for a large piece, and eighteen gauge for the enamels, and if etched in champlevé, use sixteen to even fourteen gauge.

It is the tradition to gold-plate all parts which are in contact with relics or the host. Over wood, leaf gilding would do, or a metal case, inserted, which is gold-plated. Even for wordly objects it would be very wise to have the inside treated preciously.

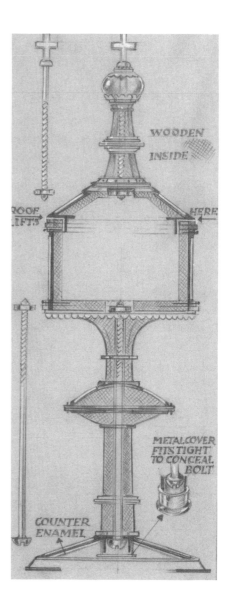

Chapter Twelve
Two Precious Boxes
Enamelled All Over

Both have much in common: the basic metal construction, the gins enamelling always presents us with, and both boxes carry some serious messages of old.

Goldpyx with Papal Insignia

(Owned by Mr. Ch. Stillman)

This is a Pyx with the papal insignia on its lid and papal blessings engraved inside, visible through transparent enamel.

Metal work

For the bottom part, the metal used is eighteen gauge thick, eighteen-carat, N-T gold.

I started with a strip of gold for the side of the box and bent it to a ring.

A. The seam had to be very neat, with as little solder on the outside as possible. The seam and the inside of the box to be buffed and polished while they could be reached so easily.

B. I soldered this ring vertically to a gold disk, leaving one millimeter overhang. **B** will become the upper rim. I inscribed a line parallel to the outside around the disk, the distance from its outside being wide enough to provide for an inside-overhang, for protection of the inside enamel and future last fitting of the lid, and I sawed along this line with a fine sawblade.

C. The smaller cut out disk was rolled in all direction to be just large enough to become the bottom of the box, plus the one millimeter added width for the protecting rim of the enamel.

D. It was domed slightly to avoid warping.

E. *It is later to be soldered to the vertical part.*

The lid of the box is made in a similar manner but with a bezel.

F. To fit it perfectly, I held it over the rim and, upside down, inscribed a line around the underside of the lid, added witness marks to be sure, and then soldered the fitted rim to it.

G. Finally I had to add a square wire as a foot and for the protection of the bottom enamel.

All that was left to do was to provide for eight hair-fine round wire loops, through which the rim of pearls was threaded and held in place. I drilled minute holes, close to the bezel, barely accommodating the wire; then I bent the wires into loops, fitted them into the metal surface, and soldered both ends safely into place. The wires, still visible on the underside of the lid, were filed off so that they could not be seen or felt anymore.

The un-enamelled cover of the pyx was sent to an engraver who cut the words of a papal blessing for the owner on its inside.

Enamelling:

The Box Part

With silver, blues, and all transparents except for reds, pinks, orange, and purples this would have been easy. I would have made two enamels, and set them back to back into a bezel—child's play! But here I had precious N-T gold and only problem colors: salmon pink, and purple.

A freshly ground coat of flux for silver was sifted over the inside, the outside, and the underside of the box. After firing I set the cloisonné wires around the vertical outside, fitting them carefully to the overlapping gold rims. Again, to reduce critical firings to a minimum, I set all letters into tightly packed enamel with a drop of glue on top of each section, and fired it. It needed two more firings, stoning in between, and considering the darkening of pink enamels in each firing, I sifted a very even coat of salmon pink over the inside only at the very last step.

The Lid

Both sides of the lid had to be perfect. I fired a thin coat of silver flux (freshly ground and washed) over the engraved inside of the lid. Then I did the same on the top, but added a thin coat of purple, and fired not too hot. The added purple would keep the color evenly—no tiny golden freckles firing through. I added pure gold and silver where the keys and tiara were to be, and set the wires right on top of the dry, pressed-on foil. Then I packed *moist*, not wet, enamel at the same time and, to save on firings, fired all.

Next, I set the wires on the inside of the lid—a small twig—on the thin coat of silver flux (remember, 25 percent of N-T gold is silver!) and fired very carefully, to hold the cloisons in place. I cut a stencil of the twig from tissue paper, glued it over the twig and sifted the pink over the rest of the surface. After removing the stencil, the leaves and berries got a wetpacked gold enamel and a hue of green.

Before the next and hopefully final firing of the inside, I could stone very gently and concentrate on finishing the top side, place the tiny gold-grains, and fire fast and hot to achieve perfect evenness and transparency.

There was some oxidation and discolorations of the metal. I could not immerse the finished piece into acid or Sparex because some enamels might be sensitive to it without a protection. All enamelled areas, therefore, were painted with asphaltum to avoid problems. Kerosine washes the asphaltum off and for the last polishing masking tape was glued over the enamel.

The pearls were strung on a very thin gold wire. Where the two ends met, they were twisted and hidden under the pearls.

The Other Box

(Owner: Professor Doctor Wolfgang Klose)

MAKING·THE·SILVERBOX

FIRST:THE·WIDE·RIM

THEN·ASSEMBLE·ALL·PARTS

SOLDER·FINISH·ENAMEL

This box is enamelled on fine silver with gold cloisonné, and was commissioned by an art lover who gave me all the freedom possible. Its theme is religious too, and legible in gold cloisonné on the very underside. All I knew about this gentleman was that he is a professor of some special science. The leading thought of this rather amusing small thing reads:

Better is a hand full of quiet than two hands full of toil
and running after the wind

(Ecclesiastes 4/6)

The drawing answers the questions of its construction. The *philosophical* approach to the small box on silver with cloisonné is indeed very different from Section 12.1. Just enjoy the five motifs, all tongue-in-cheek symbols for the blessing of repose and the joy of life.

No wind...

...he jumps out of his old gears and wants the atom...

...pulling hard on a load of books, but the wreath of laurel beckons above his head...

...he does not see the beauty at his feet.

Chapter Thirteen
Objects Representing Distinguished Offices

The staff for the Provost of the University of Connecticut and two Presidential Chains for northeastern universities will be good examples for showing construction and enamelling.

Several times I have been honored with commissions to think up and make precious objects. It might be of some interest to craftsmen how my mind worked: These chains not only have to hold the insignia of all colleges connected with the university, but also quite substantial pendants. Presidents wear robes at celebrations which remind one of the Renaissance. A heavy chain with a very heavy medallion would not be right. It has to be like a collar, staying in place on the shoulders.

To fit it onto the president I prepared a paper pattern in my studio and took it to his office, just like a tailor would have. It took a moment of polite conversation to convince him that this was necessary as a first step, but it also took only a moment to fit and I had learned what I needed to know.

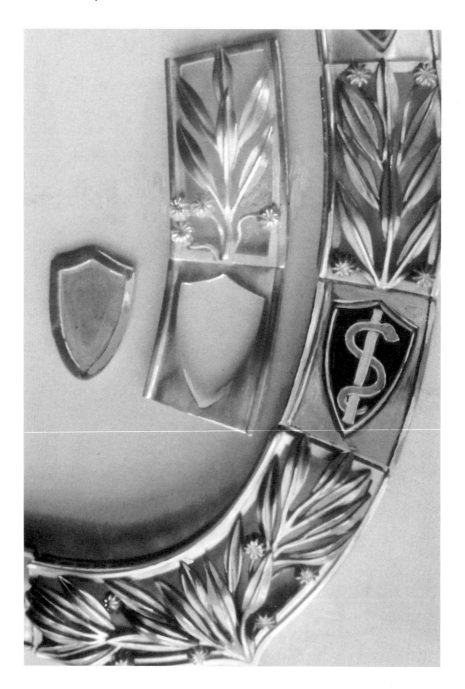

Back in my shop, I improved upon the pattern, divided it into enough sections to accommodate for the many college insignia, and the metal work could begin. The finished piece had to adjust itself to the curves of shoulders, stay in place, and move well. Except for the centerpiece in front, the sections were identical and cast from one model I very carefully made, providing for all in-between connections. This model makes it also possible to add links if the university includes more colleges.

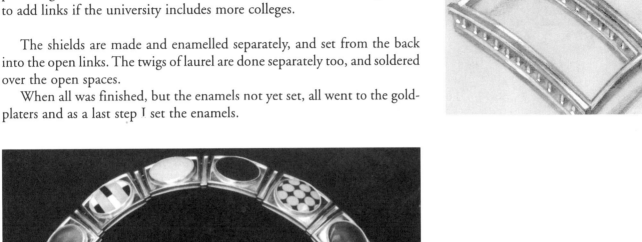

The shields are made and enamelled separately, and set from the back into the open links. The twigs of laurel are done separately too, and soldered over the open spaces.

When all was finished, but the enamels not yet set, all went to the gold-platers and as a last step I set the enamels.

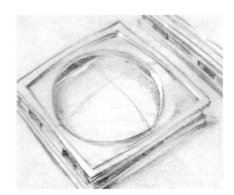

The chain for the president of Connecticut University is different in design but constructed on the same principles.

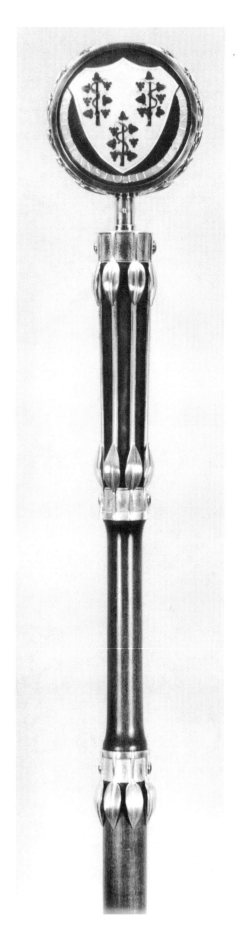

The Staff for the Provost

It is always like this: One special person is the center of merits, of influence and deep respect, and maybe of power, for good reasons. To be noticed in a group, he needs a kind of precious exclamation mark, visible from afar. In very early days in South America, VIPs had some headband combined with a long straight vertical, which could not be overlooked—of pure gold, of course.

Our democratic minds prefer the tall staff the provost of the university holds.

Here is the description of how I made the staff for Connecticut University:

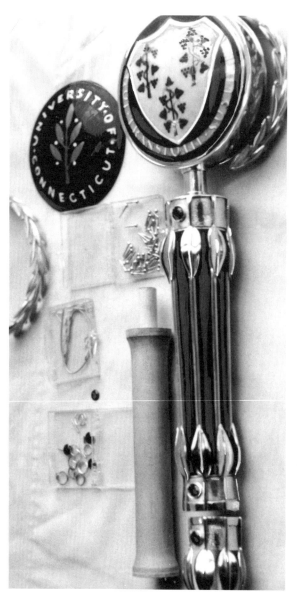

The picture shows the different parts this quite impressive piece is made of: one domed medallion about four-and-three-quarter inches in diameter on each side, gold cloisonné on fine silver, some gold foil under the enamel set into a deep bezel, all resting on a wooden spacer.

The wreath of laurel is not only symbolic for Connecticut but it keeps the silver to the wooden core inside. Where there are screws visible, their heads are nicely filed into an ornament or they sit inside silver bezels, covered with small domes of clear blue, which give the impression of stones.

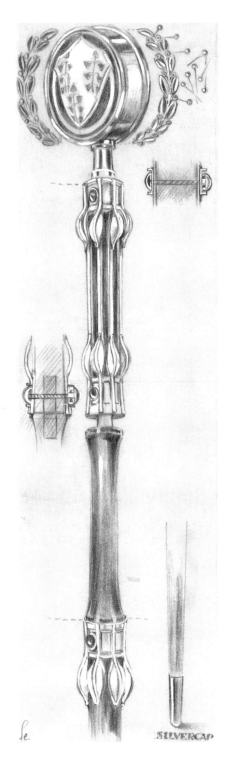

SILVERCAP

Chapter Fourteen
Candelabra with Nine Candles

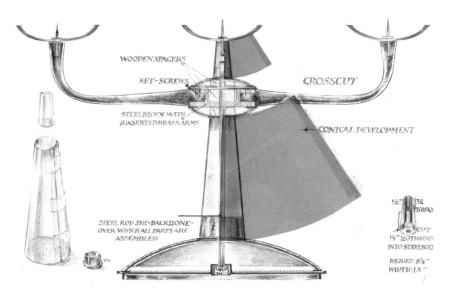

This is made of gold-plated copper and enamel.

Owned by Hans Zeitner

The theme

The nine muses, eternally young Greek goddesses who represent the arts and science—from music to poetry, history, tragedy, theatre, and astronomy. It was inviting to translate all of these into a joyous centerpiece for a festive table. A tree of lights, of enlightenment, was the half-conscious idea: with roots, a trunk, and a crown of gilt branches. Such immaterial feelings were to be translated into metal construction and enamels.

I started with four drawings:

1. proportions and all-over appearance;
2. the metal construction and details;
3. the exact line drawing for the cloisonné wires; and
4. over a pencil sketch of this design (photocopies will do even better), water colors are used to achieve a well-balanced harmony of tones.

The foot

A disk of seven-and-one-half-inches (eighteen-and-one-half-centimeters) provides the space for the enamel. Since this candelabra was meant to be a teaching and demonstration piece, I have enough slides and sketches to demonstrate better than words can do. The copper for the disc is eighteen gauge thick, which is about one millimeter and the wire used is also one millimeter high.

The branches

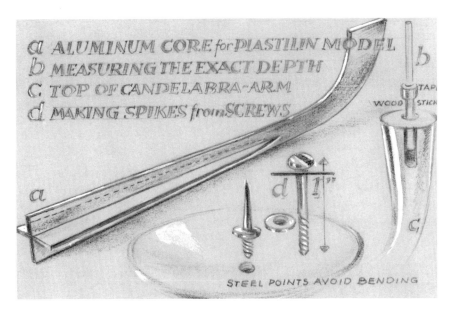

One of the eight arms, called *branches* before, is carefully modelled, first with plasticene over a skeleton of aluminum sheet, then cast in bronze. This first bronze cast is filed and formed to a perfect model for the eight cast arms. The photography and illustrations show the process. The polished arms are mounted into a heavy brass ring and held in place with set screws.

Nine small disks underneath the candles are raised, center-drilled, and provided with a thread, which is continued inside the arms. Candlelight at about eye level makes people beautiful. The piece must have a wide base to be safe. And the candles must be far enough apart from each other in order not to melt; dripping wax is to be caught in saucers and those can be easily removed and cleaned. I took care that the outline of the trunk continued through the nodus, the part we need to hold the eight branches.

The trunk

This should be first shaped with x-ray film, which is an excellent material and can easily be adjusted, cut, and glued with tape to give the three-dimensional appearance. The same holds for the small upper part of the trunk into which an iron core was inserted. On its lower end a hole is drilled and a thread cut into it exactly fitting the steel rod. The hole drilled on top fits the *thread* of the thorns holding the candle saucers and the candles.

These two holes **must not meet**. To measure the exact depth of a drilled hole, I use a toothpick with a tape around it.

The making of the enamelled **nodus** is self-explanatory. Finally, there is a small *thimble* which hides the head of the center bolt from the underside—the very last thing to do.

The composition provided for a division by eight but we must find room for the ninth muse. To reduce the first rather naturalistic sketches to utmost simplicity I used good, clear tracing paper, one on top of the other, getting the sketches down to a few lines, which are still lively, even amusing. I can push the single nine sketches of figures into the best position, fasten them with tape, and I almost ready to enjoy—let us say—three days of intensively bending and setting the wires. A very light outline with a Stabilo avoids misplacements.

The line design is traced, sketched on paper, or photocopied to place the colors—water colors at this moment.

Enamelling

We are ready to enamel the first coat of flux.

It is a rather large round plaque and the heat has to melt the flux evenly. In a small kiln, a turning of the piece might be necessary—use a lazy Susan, covered with a fireproof screen or sheet on top of the kiln. Take the glowing enamel out, put it on the lazy Susan, give it a one-quarter turn, and put it back in. Four times! It sounds much worse than it is.

After all the cloisons have been bent and set, the moment of utter concentration has come: To put the piece into the kiln without any shaking. We have spoken about this when the Family Cup was to be fired. We have flux but *no* colors yet. It is removed from the kiln still glowing red and the wires are gently pressed down to make sure they are all in.

Copper wires will be covered with cinder but the answer is the acid bath. Under running water, glass brush with a drop of ammonia first to neutralize. The piece looks now so appealing that one is tempted to leave it just as it is.

But we are to enamel, to wetpack many layers in many firings. The same procedure with less demanding design applies to the two bowl shapes which form the nodus.

There is a line of German poetry around the lower part of the nodus. In English it would read: *Oh gracious art, I thank you.* In German it reads: *Du holde Kunst, ich danke dir.*

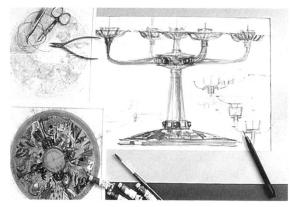

Sketch of a piece to be—line designs for shaping the cloisonné wires and a color scheme are done in advance.

The metal work begins. This will be the enamelled disk at the foot. The center and rim protect the enamel-to-be from pressure (center) and damage around the outside.

The enamel will rest in the base which holds the housing for the head of the bolt. Its rim is held in place with wire clamps—the solder is always placed where it is either not visible or can be easily filed off. Never under enamel-to-be.

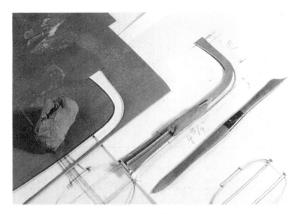

The arms: First, to find the proportion, use an improvised cutout from x-ray film, then two identical patterns from thin aluminum sheet, stuck together to hold the *plasticene*, packed around it for a generous rough three-dimensional model...

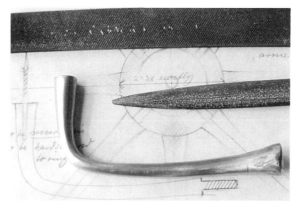

...which was cast in bronze. This rough model was then filed and shaped, reduced to polished elegance, and cast in gold-colored bronze ten times. It was cast ten times to have reserve, in case one cast was not good enough, or pores or faults (none had, to praise the caster).

The construction drawing will help to understand the following five illustrations:

According to the x-ray pattern, the *trunk* is soldered. The iron insert, fitting into its bottom, is drilled in the center to admit the steel rod.

A steel bolt, filed to fit the small copper cone, is drilled and provided with two different threads: one to fit the top of the threaded steel rod, and one to admit the smaller screw, to keep the domed disks in place.

Start to tap. Measure the correct depth with a wooden stick. The two holes must *not* meet.

Repeat the same procedure for the one-eighth-inch, thirty-two small threads on top.

The drilled bolt screwed onto the one-quarter-inch, twenty threads of the steel rod, fitting inside the cone. A one-eighth-inch, thirty-two thread screw in the upper hole.

Making the copper parts for the nodus.

Flux is sifted on the two visible sides of the nodus. Counter enamel over the insides. Pack it tightly under the rims to avoid cracks on the outsides!

Color-sketch

At last enamel work on the large disk can begin with separating the line design of the nine figures to be bent with cloisonné wires, and the color sketch, which places the colors harmoniously.

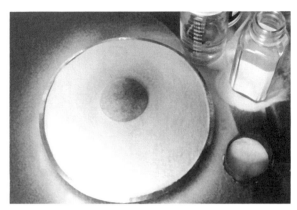

The underside has a coat of fired counter enamel. The front is carefully cleaned with Sparex, and glass brush and flux #426 is sifted, keeping center and rim unfluxed.

The division into eight sections and a light outline of one figure are made with a Stabilo pencil. And wire bending has begun.

All wires are set and fired to sink slightly into the flux...

...enamel wetpacking of the first coat begins...

...and is done over the whole surface.

The piece barely fits into the kiln—to fire it evenly, it has to be removed three times very quickly and put in again.

The nodus *happens* like kind of a sideline.

Coat over coat of enamel are wetpacked and fired to achieve...

...the desired hues in color, and especially the three-dimensional appearance—see the bodies of the muses.

Stoning is done not only to free the wires from enamel but to bring out the highlights which are the top of the relief-like packed opaques under transparent enamels.

The work seems all right.

Polishing on the wheel finishes the metalwork. Afterwards the piece is washed with soap and ammonia to remove all traces of polishing compound.

Part I of the construction drawing is permanently soldered into the cone, which is still open on top.

To check and re-check that this one stays in place, it is held with tape on the enamel. Provide witness marks inside and underneath.

We see that the trunk cone has a sturdy insert in the tip, with an opening for the rod. The insert is made from heavy pewter, while the center of the brass rim holding the eight arms is of steel. Visible on this picture are the eight set screws preventing any movement of the arms.

In drilling and thread-cutting each of the eight arms, we proceed exactly like on the small cone.
1. *pilot hole*
2. *drill smaller than thread*
3. *cut thread*

To protect the metal, the arms are resting in a sheet of lead between the jaws of a vice.

While polishing the piece, it is held with a soft cloth and clean gloves to avoid finger prints.

All parts are assembled over the central steel rod to measure the exact heights. By now the rod has the head of a strong screw soldered to its bottom end.

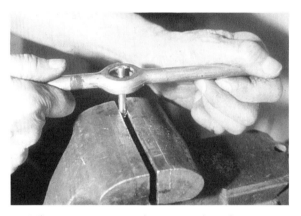

The one-quarter-inch twenty threads are cut into the upper end of the rod.

To ease the pressure and keep the center rod from moving, three small round wooden spacers are fitted and placed.

All parts fit and are ready for gold-plating.

The nine saucers to catch the wax of the nine candles are added as the last step.

Good to know:

These immortal ladies were daughters of Zeus, the President of the Gods on Mount Olympus in Greece. To say it without tongue-in-cheek, they are truly lovely symbols of the arts, and when the challenge is to express yourselves—or your patrons of art—they will help.

The names and specialties of the nine muses are:

Polyhymnia   Sacred and lyric hymns

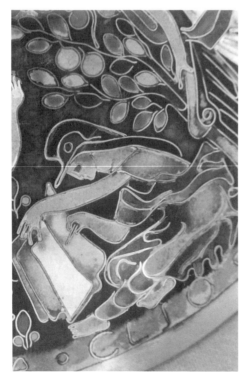

Clio   History

Calliope   Heroic poetry

Euterpe   Lyric and folks song

Erato   Poetry and music of love

Melpomene   Tragedy

Urania   Stars, space, the supernatural

Terpsichore   Dance, choral song

Thalia   Theatre

Let me chat a little about MY nine muses and what their influence upon each other is. Quite obviously they are in an intense dispute, which has a serious, hidden meaning that I tried to give to this festive candelabra.

If a group placed in a circle can have a *head of the table*, it is certainly taken by Calliope, the Muse of Heroic Song. On one hand she holds an eagle with widespread wings—quite certainly her counterpart in the world of birds. The other hand rests on her Kithara, the forerunner of the harp.

At her right sits Melpomene, deep in mourning, her left arm leaning on a fallen Greek capital—the reason is clear.

To her left, under a laurel tree, is Clio, the Muse of History, busily putting on parchment whatever heroic actions Calliope may have inspired.

Following is Thalia, the Muse of Theater, Opera, Parades, and whatever can bring to men's eyes the grandeur of the world.

Terpsichore, the Muse of Dance, enjoys herself between Thalia and dear and sweet Erato, the Muse of Love Song, who is joining her tune with Euterpe, the Muse of Lyric and the naive, innocent folk song. So much to the left half of this enamelled piece of poetry.

Turning to the right, we have already met weeping Melpomene, who is the Muse of Tragedy, in word and music. Back to back with her, on the stump of a laurel tree, sits Polyhymnia. She writes and writes without end. Her words come like a waterfall, as she is the Muse of Epos, the great long tales every nation treasures, and the reports of the past and promises for the future. Which brings us to Urania, the Muse of the Heavens, the Stars, and Science. She floats over the oceans and reaches to the stars.

Quite a story for a candelabra which is to be in the center of my family's gatherings and will hopefully take their minds off the burdens of every day.

Chapter Fifteen
Icons for Contemplation

Chapters One to Nine contain the technical information needed to know how the objects on the following pages are physically made. What our hands produce should look easy, although it might be the result of years of learning.

The finest skill will create the finest *handcraft*, but where do we enter the domain of *fine art*?

I shall now try to stand up for what the title of this book promises: enamel as medium for fine art.

Inspiration and mature thought, both of them, surpass dexterity. But true know-how of what enamel and its innumerable possibilities can do, this know-how is the enameller's solid base, combined with sensible metal work.

Thoughts and problems, which *are in the air* do not present themselves with logic words; sometimes the catalyst is a conversation, sometimes it is pondering over a woman's place in life (see *The Perfect Lady*). Or it might be the superb beauty of a flower, compared with the human vanity to put on a glorious exterior (the *Iris panel*). Anyway, my own mind's eye translates impressions into instant images, parables, and visual symbols. It is not that I search for such, they get a hold on me. Nobody has it always!

Much of what we do is just good work. Many are inspired, but are not trained enough to put on paper or into any material what moves their imagination and mind. If sketching and sober observation becomes a habit, that is a great help. **Understanding** the inner law of the object (as if it were a living thing) or **drawing** an object the way it presents itself exercises our eyes and hands and is, indeed, fun. The pitfall for the able artist is **to overdo**!

To attain that *simplicity which says it all*, one must peel away all dispensable details and become saturated only with the essence and hope. In the case of cloisonné, that means that the few inches of wire or line drawing express what one aims for. It is almost like a miracle if a slide of one's work, enlarged on a big screen, speaks out what we felt.

I leave it now to you, my readers and co-enamellers, to criticize and to improve on your own work where I may have failed.

Joseph, Who Was Sold by His Brothers

(Owned by Mr. and Mrs. Daniel Dibner)

Plaque size seven-inches-by-seven-inches.

Made of copper cloisonné, the theme is thousands of years old and could be today's as well.

Santa Barbara

(Owned by Professor Dr. M. Hagenkötter Dortmund)

Her left hand points to the bitter chalice, while her...

She protects the men in the mines
and is the helper in thunderstorm and
mining catastrophes.

...right hand seems to bring consolation, help, and blessing.

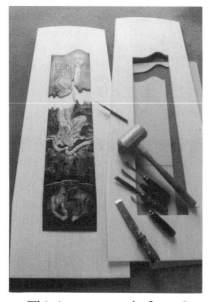

This icon was made for a German mining district. The plaque size is about four feet high, and it is made of copper cloisonné.

The Final Step

(owned by Peter N. Zeitner)

Man takes the daring step to leave his earthboundness and enter the unknown. He strives for the nucleus of the atom, the unmeasurable energy of cosmos. But he steps on a cloud—will it hold him safe or will he, misusing energy and science take a deep fall?

Man's Footprints

(Owned by Hans Zeitner)

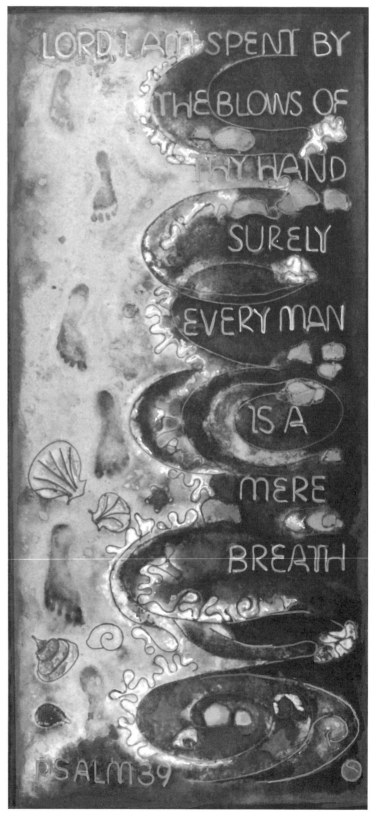

The next wave will wash them away.

Children of All Colors

(Owned by Christopher Zeitner)

Made for the Year of the Child of Unesco. The words in its separately enamelled frame read: *Whoever receives such a child receives me*, Matthew 18:5.

The Perfect Lady

(Owned by Ms. Cele Peterson)

In daytime she is—well, you see for yourself—charming and reserved. In night she is a garden of flowers.

Iris

This is the study from nature of an iris, a lily of the fields.

The queen of the irises it is, inspired by a place of extreme elegance and luxury. The words on top and bottom of the cloisonné read: *Solomon in all his glory, was not arrayed like one of these*. This panel also shows the free translation into cloisonné, pure gold foil fired underneath the enamel, and goldgrains.

An enlarged detail.

E=mc²

(Owned by Lukas Zeitner)

The formula of Einstein which states the fact: **All is energy**...all is what we cannot name. Logos was the Greek word, but it is not only the word, it is the power, it is what the Far Eastern philosophers named **Tao**. The Hebrew symbol, the letter *J*, stands for God, another name for what cannot be named. In the center of the deep blue, material forms from the eternal, immortal energy.

Unisono

(Owned by the Museum of Fine Arts, Boston)

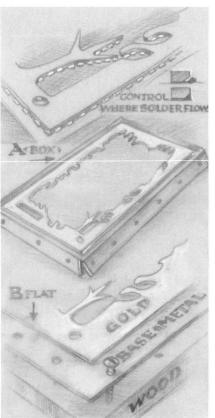

Unisono means the complete oneness of mind and nature. To comprehend this taught me a great lesson. Indeed, there is suffering, but there is also delight and joy. One may have to grow quite old to gratefully accept Unisono.

Anyway, here are **Pan**, the Greek god of nature and **Erato**, the muse of love songs, dancing over a meadow red with poppies. One sunny day on the Greek island of Samos filled me with the inspiration for this panel. Everything had deep meaning and the restrained beauty of the bare essentials: Red poppies are not just lovely flowers, but they symbolize dream, love, and death. There were tall plants looking like evil itself: One dark purple wrapped around a tall black pistil. Hundreds-of-year-old olive trees of grayish-green, and in a tiny valley, shaded by trees, the reflection of water and rocks, framing the perfect idyl, and stillness.

Forgetting myself, my pencil scribbled on some piece of paper what moved me, and the scribbles took shape and brought the image to life.

Pan, son of Hermes and the nymph Penelope, was born hairy and with goat feet. His mother did not really want him, but his father Hermes wrapped him into the pelt of a hare and took him up to the residence of the Greek gods on Mount Olympus. The gods delighted in his liveliness and raised him. So much for his mythical background.

While I hope that my tale finds a resonance in you, my readers, let me give some sober facts about how to make a piece like this. It is eighteen carat N-T gold, about one millimeter thick. The outline of the design is sawn out with utter care with a very fine sawblade. Several tiny holes were drilled previously along the contour to have easy access.

The gold was then soldered on a flat, eighteen gauge sheet of metal. It could be gold, fine silver, or copper. If it had been a small plaque I would have used the T&D method, but with an object three-inches-by-six-inches, I wanted to be absolutely certain of its perfection. The carrier metal is about one-and-one-half-inches bigger than the gold on top. Its edges are bent down to form a small box which stabilizes the piece in the many firings to come, and provides space for counter enamel and setting into its frame without problems.

The cloisonné wires are hair-fine and slightly higher than the sheet of gold in which they sit to avoid deep spots when all enamel has been filled in and the surface is to be stoned.

How many firings? I guess about six or seven.

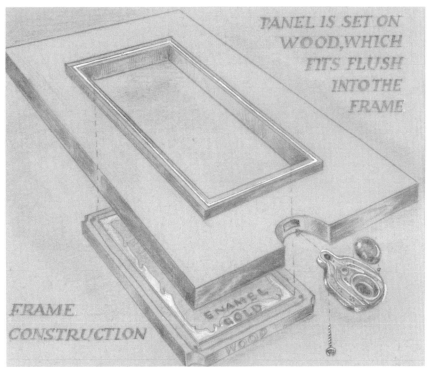

The wooden frame by Gorden Merrick had to be as precious, though understated, as the enamel itself.

The finished piece.

Nota Bene

A word, tongue-in-cheek, about finished enamelled mishaps: They do not self-destruct—somebody will dig them out!

Chapter Sixteen
Gold-Grain Enamel

The preceding chapter was, indeed, what today's young might call *heavy stuff*. From drawing with the exactness of a camera to forgetting it and translating the observed into abstract lines of metal, from soul-searching to the most sober reductions of one's precious emotions, we are now ready for a very light and elegant dessert after a heavy meal: gold-grain enamel.

In Chapter Eight you found the description of how to produce the tiny gold spheres, how to sift them into similar sizes, and that N-T gold is the ideal metal to use.

Let us talk about the enamelled metal base: If affordable, eighteen carat N-T gold would be the ideal carrier. The price is higher than copper, indeed, but the value of a finished enamel surpasses that difference tenfold. Silver under shockproof blue transparents is alright. For a larger piece, copper serves very well if its surface is acid-cleaned, shiny, and engraved with a florentine engraving tool for more reflection.

The surface holds at least two evenly sifted and fired coats of transparent enamel, **no flux**, and is stoned to perfection. By now the enamel is quite thin, which is what we want. After thoroughly washing it, it is refired fast and hot to a flawless gloss.

With a fine paintbrush and glue (Klyr-Fire) the grains are set. To dry them fast, I work closely under a hot lightbulb. If the placement of the grains has to be secured on a certain spot, one may grind tiny indentations for each into the enamel. A dentist's diamond-impregnated round drill will do. When firing, hold your breath and catch the enamel by surprise—very fast and **hot**—it gets tacky instantly and the grains have no chance to roll off. Since the enamel surface is thin, the grains cannot sink in deep and drown any more than one-quarter of their diameter.

For examples, here are three different shapes and sizes: a small plaque two inches in diameter with the three graces (Aglaia, the festive charme; Euphrosyne, cheerfulness; and Thalia, for a happy life).

a) a small plaque

b) grains of gold on a blue transparent sphere (a sample)

c) gold grains are part of the gold cloisonné design and are freely placed to
    suggest the unbelievable beauty of an iris; it seems as though the inside
    were powdered with gold dust.

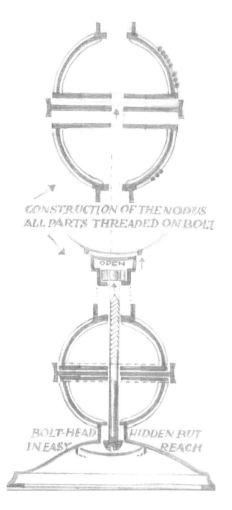

CONSTRUCTION OF THE NODUS
ALL PARTS THREADED ON BOLT

OPEN

BOLT-HEAD HIDDEN BUT
IN EASY REACH

The shaping and enamelling of a sphere to become the nodus of an eighteen carat golden Kiddush Cup (N-T Gold).

1. Make a pattern of thin aluminum sheet with which to check the symmetry of the two semi-spheres.
2. These two half-spheres are raised from non-tarnishing metal twenty gauge thick, either in a dapping die or over a stake. They must be identical.
3. Have the nut and bolt available which will hold the entire cup together when it is assembled. The size of this nut determines much of the metalwork. You may have to change the outer shape of the nut.
4. Solder the two half-spheres on rims wide enough to protect the inside and the outside and provide sturdy guidance for the bolt.
5. Depending on the material with which you are working, construct a small open case of gold or silver for the nut. This case is not soldered to the half-spheres but is to be part of the raised cup, as the drawing shows. But it has to be constructed before the metal work of the half-spheres can be finished. Cut a hole into the bottom of the case just large enough to permit the bolt to pass through and then solder the nut into its housing.
6. A gold ring (collar) fitting exactly over the nut housing, has been soldered over the center of the bottom of the cup part. The nut housing is to be **soft** soldered, with pewter solder in this exceptional case, inside this collar. The large surface of its upper cover permits enough contact to hold safely.
7. The two semi-spheres are ready for enamelling after the usual pickling and cleaning. You will need one more bezel and a small enamel to hide the bolt at the bottom of the cup. Though it can be seen only when the cup is turned upside down, this piece should be prepared with the same care as any small plaque.

A few words remain to be said about firing the round gold grains on glossy half-spheres and keeping them in place: Of course, the glue burns off the moment the pieces are put into the hot kiln, but—so I thought—if the kiln is almost white hot, it might work. I should catch the grains by surprise, sticking them to the enamel before they can fall off. It did work.

My commission was to make two identical cups for two scientists exploring **space**. They are brothers and the cups were gifts from their parents. To find the leading thought was left to me. I had time to let it happen, to wait. And it happened: I was thumbing through the biblical book of the psalms. In Psalm 19, I read:

The Heavens proclaim the glory of God and the firmament is his handiwork.

These words are engraved around the nodus and the foot. Ancient truth and as new as the day tomorrow.

Chapter Seventeen
A Large Frame Set with Grisaille Enamels and Semi-precious Stones

There was a different challenge on my mind when I made this frame: To work out a method to create precious book covers like those of earlier centuries. It seemed foolish to make such a one without the book to be clad. However, I was intrigued to find my own technical approach. It became a mirror which is now a jewel on a light colored wall, the accent of a modern home. A joy to the eye and a solution to my task.

The enamels are painted **grisaille** on a clean blue transparent enamel. If it were that precious book I would have used an enamel technique even more precious, something like cloisonné or champlevé.

How is it all put together, the size and width of the frame, the exact measurements of the twenty separately made parts, and how they would fit without any gaps or visible screws? The width of the frame determines the three-dimensional squares and the length of each of the ten bezels holding the enamels. The basic core is wood, covered with polished brass. It must be easy to take all pieces apart for repairs and reassemble without problem or glue.

Drawing number four in Chapter Four describes the making of the squares. Stones, set into soldered-on bezels, hide the screws which hold everything safely together. It is because of these screws that I had to add stones. The shapes alone are ready for setting without any soldering. The copper used is 20 gauge, which is 0.75 millimeters, gold-plated.

The copper rectangles to be enamelled and counter enamelled are 22 gauge, or 0.5 millimeters, their edges are bent down, and they fit comfortably into the bezels which are also made of 22 gauge copper, later gold-plated. Each has about five millimeter overhang on the small sides, while the long sides are finished smoothly. The grisaille technique is explained in Chapter Nine.

Loosely screw on the corner squares and slide the small side of the rectangular bezels underneath the squares. Fasten the screws. Continue all the way around the frame. These screws go through the brass cover and deep into the wooden core.

Use tiny screws or thin nails to hold the rectangular bezels in place and set them deep with a punch.

All is ready for the finishing touches: cut small leather rings to surround all screws and avoid any damage to the stones to be set now.

The same holds for enamels. They, too, rest on leather. All is done. The mirror is placed and fastened from the back, covered with either very thin plywood or with leather, or in any other manner to hold it safely.

An afterthought: If this had been the precious book cover, all work would be mounted on very dry, specially made thin plywood.

The exact design on adhesive paper is glued on eighteen gauge copper.

The holes drilled just permit the saw blade.

The saw blade is as wide as the copper imprint is thick.

All parts are cut out. Two for the center for oval and square stones. The first imprints are made for the oval and the square.

With the T&D the ten final squares for the stones are produced without soldering. The bezels for the stones can now be soldered in place.

Over a steel plate three sides are bent up. The fourth remains almost flat until the hard board is inserted.

The steel plate is replaced with a hard board square; the four sides are bent over it, and after gold-plating a center hole was drilled.

Bezels for the enamels were already made. In mounting all parts on the frame, they slide underneath the squares.

Holes for small nails were already drilled through bezels and brass.

After all rectangles were placed, drilled, and nails set deep with a punch; the center screws, holding the squares, are tightened.

Inserts of pieces of leather, thick enough to avoid the screws scratching the stones, are put into each bezel.

The enamels, too, are fitted and set over leather. The stones are set into place.

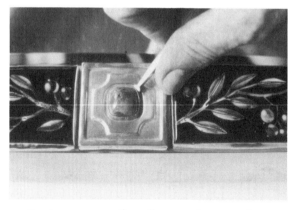

Setting a stone after all mounting was done.

The oval stones are set at the four corners.

Chapter Eighteen
Bishop's Cross and Bishop's Ring

What a beautiful responsibility: To translate deep thought into the most precious and most lasting of materials. Whenever possible, I give my work two front sides, each having its own message.

Twenty-two carat gold for the cloisonné and the cross, and the small enamel under a flat amethyst in the ring. Eighteen carat gold for the ring.

The arms of the crucified man reaching from Alpha, the beginning, to Omega, the end. His feet are entangled in the very earthly, his mind is rising into the spiritual. The bishop trusted me enough to let me choose the words for the other side, words I have used repeatedly, because they are true to all religions, although here expressed in the Gospel of John 6:63:

It is the spirit that gives life. The flesh is of no avail. The words that I have spoken to you are spirit and life.

The Ring

A thinly cut amethyst is covering a very small gold cloisonné five-eighths-inch-by-four-eighths-inch, *The man who helps to carry the cross.* His biblical name was Simon from Cyrena. I call him *the friend.* The symbols of a bishop's office are engraved left and right on the wide shank of this ring: two fish and the bishop's hat.

The bishop's ring is a band, wide in front, slim in back, comfortable to wear—yet not a piece of embellishment, but rather to distinguish the sacred office of its bearer.

Amethyst is the traditional stone. Here it is ground and polished to a thin slice.

The Cross

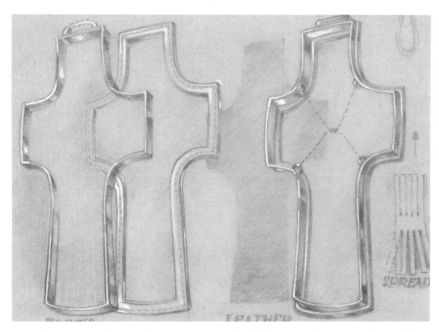

The construction of the cross: two identical cross-shapes, with gold rims to hold the enamel safely, were prepared and enamelled.

One cloisonné for the front, one for the back. Only after both were finished, could the golden setting be made. The two wires inside the gold cross reinforced its stability. The leather softens the contact of metal with counter enamel, wires, and frame.

The chain is led through a link made from a rectangular piece of gold, one millimeter thick. See illustration.

Enlarged head of Christ; the original size of it is one-half-inch.

Chapter Nineteen
Book of Gospels

Two book covers for a New Testament.

It began years ago with the gold enamels for a small altar. The man who commissioned me to make the nine panels was fascinated by the dignity of ancient Byzantine gold cloisonné. He believed that I could do those, but my reply had to be, "Maybe I can do New York-Byzantine enamels of the twentieth century." Ages later I wondered what had become of that altar. It had been taken to Austria and stayed there for a long time; the enamels had been removed by someone and glued, like stamps on a letter, to the leather binding of an old book. At the time of my questioning, this book was back in the United States of America in a small monastery in the southwestern desert.

Non-tarnishing gold is quite soft and must not be exposed to daily rough handling. If so, it has to be set deep into rims of higher metal. My concern was shared by the same patron of my art, and he trusted me with making safe changes. You see on the photographs how I solved this problem: I could not have the book sent to my studio in New England, but had to rely on the exact measurements of the eight panels and the crucifixus, sent to me by the abbot. He did the most exact job in centimeters.

My start was to cut the form of the panels from hard cardboard and place them on paper with the outlined space of the book's size; that left room for the metal work and the enamelled crosses on both sides. Front and back are slightly varying because of the different widths of the crosses. For the metal work I chose polished, silvery, non-tarnishing, and lead-free **pewter**. It has a good feel and I like it as a component to enamels. I prepared the parts, down to every bolt and nut, in my own shop, and then took all of the tools, including the flexible shaft, with me to that idyllic place outside of today's world, in the middle of nowhere.

The improvised workshop at the monastery was a table in a kind of cell which also was my living quarters. The flexible shaft dangled from a beam over my table. Except for one two-millimeter drill, I had all of the equipment for work in one small suitcase. This "no mistakes allowed" situation, the simplicity, the absence of anything ugly, the almost poverty, and the peace were ideal for total concentration. Hours did not count.

Fine silver and/or sterling silver were used in all bezels, nuts, and small enamels. Underneath the bezels for the semi-precious stones are the bolts and inside the leather binding are nicely filed nuts. The original end papers could not possibly be combined with something that would be machine made.

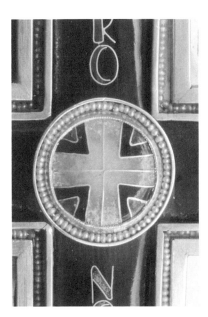
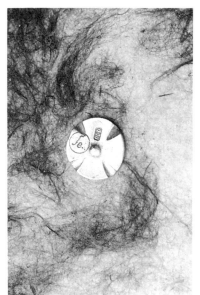

The Front Cover

The design had to provide for a cross wide enough to be the background of the existing gold cloisonné crucifix. I placed it on the super-exact *floor plan*, the size fitting the already existing book.

The cut out stencils of the size and thickness of the four gold panels determined where and how wide the beams of the cross could be. Not to forget the necessary pewter work on the width of the outer rim, into which the six bezels for the stones had to fit.

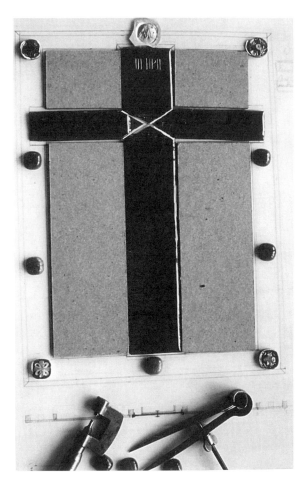

The enamelled cross consists of four parts. The vertical parts are to hold the crucifix. On x-ray film, the crucifix's exact outline was cut out, transferred to twenty gauge copper, and a T&D was sawn out. With this T&D the space for the figure could be set slightly deep. Now a sturdy two millimeter wide rim was soldered under each of the four cross parts, (not under the four triangular parts which meet in the center of the cross) providing space for the counter enamel. The design happened almost by itself. Since the crucifix fits into the provided space, the holes for the four nails were drilled into the yet un-enamelled copper. Those nails will hold the figure and the cross; four more holes at the crossing of the vertical and horizontal beams provide for a safe mounting.

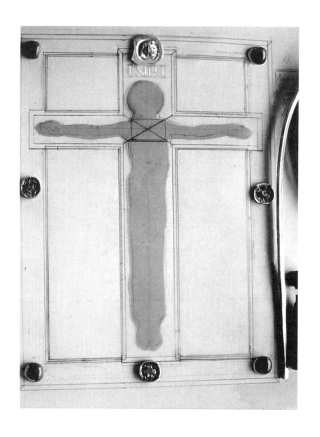

There was enough space above Christ's head for an underlay of silver: I N R I in gold cloisonné.

All new enamel work must be finished before the pewter work begins. Scalex was painted over the front of each piece first, **clear flux** 426 was sifted over the back. Flux, after the first firing, is so pliable that one can gently even it out with a mallet. Then, after cleaning, the front of each piece is first sifted with a thin coat of flux, and clean-clean blue, over it. Both are fired at the same time. Add a second coat of blue and that should be all, except over the I N R I we have to add another thin coat of blue. The openings for the nails are widened before the last firing, which is fast and hot for evenness and clarity. A diamond-impregnated burr for the opening of the holes was used. Add a drop of water for better grinding.

The Back Cover

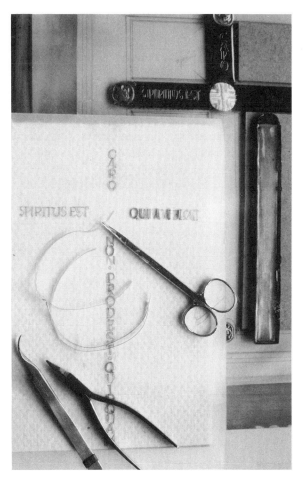

The enamels for the back cover are constructed differently: The four copper shapes, which form the cross, are built like flat, open boxes. The vertical, bent down rims, about three-millimeter one-sixteenth-inch wide, hold the pieces in shape. They are counter enamelled with plenty of flux, especially all corners in order to avoid cracks. Fired over a piece of mica to prevent enamel from dropping into the kiln, they are then flattened on an anvil with a mallet. Proceeding with the front of each: Flux plus blue is fired, then the cloisonné letters are set and held safely with some blue enamel against the outsides and the opaque lighter turquoise against the insides of the letters.

The enamel is very tightly packed and fired, not too high, then filled and re-fired, following the normal procedure. Now strips of transparent paper are cut to cover the lettering while sifting on what is, probably, the last coat of blue. It would be wise to spray Klyr-Fire first and, enamel between your fingers, salt additional blue along all edges.

The firing is to be hot and fast. Stoned and refired—and that is it. While still glowing hot, one might have to apply a bit of pressure with a long spatula to the row of letters.

The Pewter Rim

This is as high as the one around the crucifix on the front. The rims around the four enamelled plaques are the same as on the front and these enamels are also set from the back. The heights of these rims protect the enamels.

The bezels around the stones and the three medallions work exactly like the six on the front cover—as anchors that serve to connect the new pieces with the old leather binding of the book.

The Last Task

Finally, I removed all the scratches from the eight gold panels. With small brushes and the flexible shaft, with rouge and felt wheels, with endless patience and by hand, the lovely surface came back.

To Mount Both Covers

Mounting was pure joy—everything fitted and it took little adjusting. I added strings of seed pearls around the cross on the back and when I was ready to bring my work to the chapel, there stood the abbot at the top of the stairs, white silk in his hands, and he received it with a grace I will never forget. He carried the book inside to the altar, spoke a short word in Latin, and the modest room was flooded with unexpressable grace.

Chapter Twenty
Small Enamelled Sculptures of Precious Metal

A leading European master-goldsmith stated, "Nobody can enamel small gold figures anymore." I had to try it, and here are two results in different approaches.

Saint Michael

Saint Michael is constructed of different thicknesses of N-T gold wires and sheet of eighteen carat. It will not tarnish during firings, and it is soft for bending and shaping. The figure is one-and-three-eighths inches tall, the all over size is two inches.

It consists of nine parts, all fitting and provided with tiny gold nuts threaded to fit.

Illustration number two tells about soldering and filing a small figure. (The dragon was made in a similar way.)

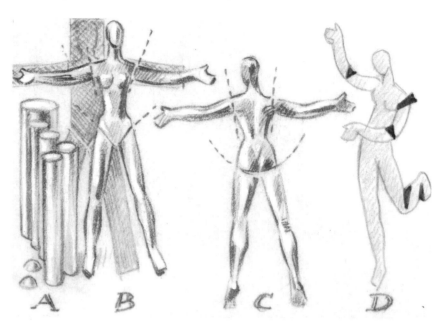

A: the five pieces of wire, and the shaded creature gives an idea of how the very rough first assembling is done.

B: the figure filed from it.

C: the backview—remember to provide for his/her bottom.

D: seems to be a cruel operation indeed: Wedges are sawn or filed where the limbs are to be bent for gracious movements. Still being bald-headed, it needs a wig: Let us make one!

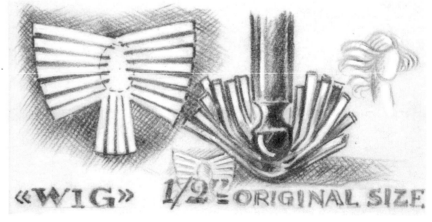

«WIG» 1/2" = ORIGINAL SIZE

To solder it to the head is a bit tricky: Standing on its head in an indentation in my charcoal block, the legs rest against another charcoal, and the hollow side of the minute wig is filled with half-molten solder. It is heated to a yellowish glow, and the wig will have become part of the sculpture. We have no tarnishing problem, but wherever the limbs have been bent and soldered into position, a drop of moist ochre will prevent mishaps. It is child's play, indeed, to shape the wig into an attractive coiffure.

Under his left foot, Michael-to-be receives a wide flat piece of gold, which will, at the final mounting, be held inside the pedestal he will stand on. Since our hero wears a Greek antique uniform for battling the dragon, I had to provide rims wherever enamel would be—his greaves, his kind of kilt, and what I call his t-shirt—all hard soldered with gold solder and without gaps, which may cause cracking in the enamel. That was no child's play.

To safely enamel on such tight and curvy spaces, the cloisonné wires were set right onto the gold. Some were held with bits of solder, some were just tightly packed with a drop of glue on top. As a trivet I made him a couch of iron wire which supported him well and touched **only** spots which are **gold**, not enamel. All spots in his limbs where solder might open got a touch of ochre.

Having a first coat of enamel secure the lower half, I bent the wires which would safely hold and avoid cracking in his "shirt." Those curves of the body had to be divided as the ornament is not decoration only.

A second coat of turquoise is packed up to the gold rims. I know it looks unproportioned, but all wires and rims must be imbedded into molten glass. Blue was chosen for the upper part. Blues are safe, as far as there is safety.

With wet carborundum and a small carborundum wheel in a flexible shaft, Saint Michael got his manly slim figure and was ready for mounting. To enamel and fire the dragon was easy. His scales, engraved deep enough to hold the small amounts of transparent enamel, were filled to overflow, and needed only one firing, one stoning, polishing, and a final firing to restore the clarity and shine of the enamel.

I was ready for the engineering part: The picture shows the nine parts, the interior of the small pedestal, exposes the golden wedge securing Saint Michael's foot, and the thin gold wires onto which the pearls are threaded around the outside. All that was left to do was to set the oval enamel into its bezel.

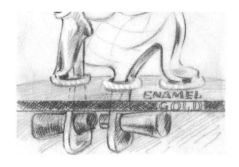

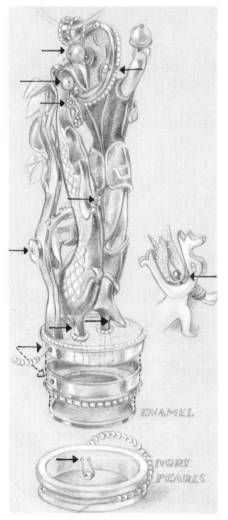

There is the cloisonné oval which will cover the bottom of the stand, and from its finished size we can calculate the size of the platform on which the dragon and figure are to be mounted. The tree-like shape on the back side is kind of a backbone, securing the dragon where a gold wire sticks out, which threads through the dragon's tail. There is a thread cut into it, so a pearl with the negative of the same thread size, could be screwed on.

The figure is secured not only by the wedge inside the stand, but also with a threaded wire in the back of its head which passes through the center of the halo and is topped with a pearl. As a third fixing point, the wire on the right foot (which has been threaded) passes through a small hole and receives a gold nut.

The sword fits tightly into a drilled hole in the mouth of the dragon after it passes through Saint Michael's hand. A pearl again tops it. The granulated dragon's tongue, which has a soft gold wire with a granule on top, is stuck through and wound around one of those fantastic dragon-back spines. It sounds like and IS playful fun.

Two pins stick out from the oval base. These pins are securing the exact fit of the two box parts. Later, the gold wire, onto which pearls are threaded, will pass through these tiny holes.

The saint may be worn on a necklace, or be enjoyed by being set into an ivory stand with pearls.

The Miracle of the Sea

(Owned by Professor Doctor W. Klose)

Let me tell you about a completely different approach to a small piece of sculpture to be worn as a jewel. Its theme is inspired by an engraving by Albrecht Dürer: "The Miracle of the Sea," a merman and his human love.

To begin with, I modelled plasticene over a skeleton of iron wire. It was a rough idea of shape and size. The next step, a cast in plaster of Paris. That made a few more details possible, and was then cast in **pewter**. Pewter, a soft metal, permitted fine filing and polishing and is an excellent material for models to be cast in precious metal, as long as they are not soft soldered and open in the process of making a rubber mold.

A good engraver cut the scales into a final silver model. The arms of the two figures are strong enough and small enough to be bent for any expression or to hold whatever the desired symbol might be.

Our merman holds a shield, and his girl has a horn of plenty in her arm, both attached the way humans would hold them. Both attributes are made separately and are not cast.

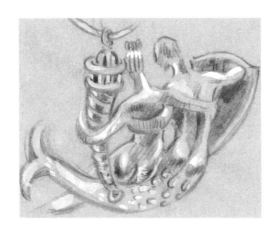

Chapter Twenty-one
Five Panels

Silver cloisonné set into black wood.

These five panels are the results of living through the wrongs of World War II and contemplating what made it happen, indeed a very profound theme. The figures of the Bible offer, in their symbolism, parallels to those traps mankind fell, and still falls, into: betrayal, apathy, violence, and greed. The center panel shows the silent discussion between the man on the cross and the one sitting under it, on a scorched window cross, fallen from one of the ruins in the background.

The five panels are executed with silver closionné. Time is darkening the shiny wires and that is good. To translate the original pencil designs and sketches into wires is my way to achieve that concentrated expression in a few lines which I am unable to do in painting. To say what I had to say needed a language which everybody who has eyes to see and has ever had contact with the New Testament will absorb. These panels are not illustrations of the Gospels.

Panel 1: Betrayal

...obviously for personal gain. Jesus' gesture says what the Bible tells us—"My friend, what are you doing?"—compassion with the one who burdens himself with evil.

Panel 2: Apathy

...to escape responsibility, to remain silent and blind in the face of horror.

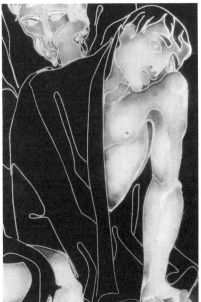

Panel 3

holds the question: "My God, **why** hast thou forsaken me?" Let the details
speak.

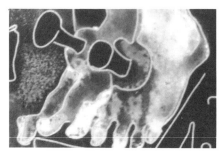

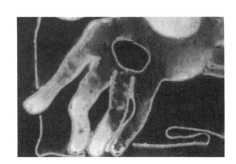

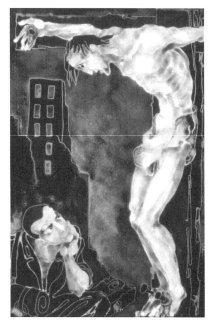

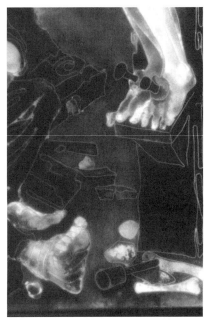

Panel 4: Violence

"Put your sword back...whoever takes up the sword will die by the sword."

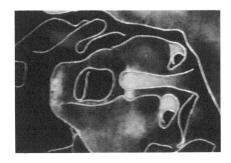

Panel 5: Greed/Materialism

The betrayer cannot live with the gain he got. He throws it away; and the generations to come pick it up and we start all over again.

What else is there to say?

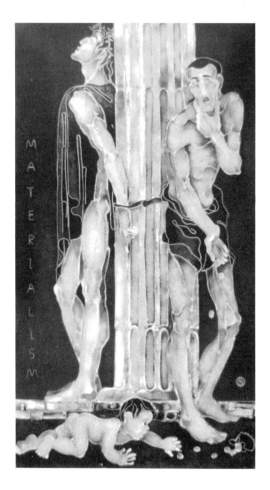

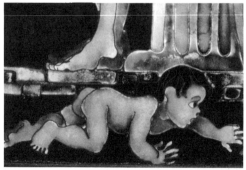

Chapter Twenty-two
Miniature Portraits

Painting enamels are also used for china painting. They are used in the same manner as grisaille. Pure gold is called **sponge** by refiners. It is mixed and fired like grisaille but must be laid on quite thickly. After firing, and glass brushing under water, it has a fine matte appearance; or for more brilliance, steel polish with a burnisher and soapy water. For small quantities ask for **Roman gold**, which comes in the shape of a small cake.

Used for special highlights, grisaille and gold may be used in combination with enamelled objects.

To give an example, painting enamel serves very well as a shading on portraits.

Elena

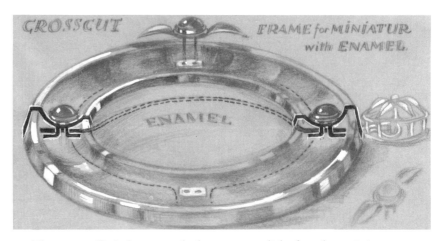

The enamelled frame and the copper disk for the miniature were prepared at the same time. The frame is spun copper, eighteen gauge thick. The disk to hold the portrait is fitting underneath the frame and will be held with four clamps which disguise their purpose under corals and small decorations.

The frame was enamelled inside and outside with a deep blue transparent. Four small *islands* are left without enamel.

The frame was finished first.

This illustration shows the domed copper part for the painting, a small jewel-like pendant to serve for the hanging of this piece, and four small clamps. The wide bare copper rim permits perfect fitting when the two pieces are permanently put together. The four ears each have two holes drilled, to receive the wires of the four clamps.

The part for the construction all being done, the painter's work may start: Mixed with about one-third of flux, a light fleshtone of opaque enamel is evenly sifted and fired. A second coat without flux is added, fired, and stoned to a perfect surface. Then a third thin coat of the same opaque is added, and fired high to get a solid and even surface. From a lifesize water-color of the model, reduced in size, drawings were made on tracing paper, to improve without losing what is good.

The portrait is sketched with vitreous painting enamels and carefully dried and fired at low heat (red glowing inside kiln).

The outer contour of Elena's head is traced on thin paper and together with paper towel carefully cut out. It is moistened with water and placed on the enamelled circle. The dark blue of the background is sifted over the round. At the same time, a small sample is developed side by side with the original.

When the paper stencil is lifted with tweezers, some blue grains might settle on the flesh tone. Removing them now avoids blemishes on the portrait.

After firing the blue, the surface is stoned once more—it is just a minute's work with a soft stone and some wet-and-dry emery paper.

Vitreous enamel painting colors are mixed with oils and have the desirable creamy consistency. The sample plaque receives a sketch of an eye. It is fired and looks all right. We now can do the whole portrait—lines, forms, and shades—some gentle coloring, no black! The firing has to be watched with care, because overfiring causes the paint to just disappear.

From now on, easy melting enamels (water-mixed enamels) are used, which is our next step: The background is improved, a brown transparent is wetpacked over the hair and the eyes, while opal white accentuates the eyeballs. It is understood that the copper is covered with Scalex before each firing, and washed off afterwards to avoid mishaps.

It is possible to work with oil-mixed enamel and water-mixed enamel at the same time, but the two must never touch....unfired, that is. Grisaille white for highlights in eyes, etc., is now added, contours are sharpened, and after firing, we are ready for the first of two sifted coats of clean, very soft flux—just a veil of it. After a mild firing, not to maturity, a second coat, and maybe at the same time some effects with pure gold (sponge or Roman gold) on the blue will pull the painted colors together. No flux over the background—brush it off. That is it. The portrait is set underneath the frame and held by the four clamps. The four corals cover the solder joints inside the bezels.

The only task left is to cover the back with fine fabric, stretched over hard board.

A Man's Portrait

Four-and-one-half-inches-by-six-and-one-half-inches can hardly be called a miniature. I had a lifesize original, whereby large size is the rule for either oil paintings or watercolors or just drawing. To fill extended space with enamels, if the task is to remain true to nature, has its problems. The same problems I have experienced with very large cloisonné panels. To fill the open spaces with interesting, lively wetpacking is an unexpected task.

It is a different matter if the design is a very free translation inspired but not copied from nature (see the Iris Panel, Chapter Fifteen). To see one's work enlarged 100 times on a big screen, and it still remains strong, alive, and is not distorted, that is what one hopes for. The technical realization of this man's image was similar to the portrait of **Elena**, except that a glossy surface would be wrong.

After all was finished and the last coat of clear flux had pulled the two different enamelling techniques into one, I treated the surface with a matting acid, let it work no longer than absolutely needed, washed it using some ammonia in the water, and after it had dried, I waxed it.

Four times enlarged, this photo shows that there are only forms in a face, no lines.

The Poet Albert Bauer

This portrait is so typical for what I wish to include into this chapter, that I discuss it again, although it might be known from my book *The Art of Enamelling*.

No flux: Two evenly sifted coats of transparent gray. Number 122 from Vienna is an enamel which does not crack and heals again during firing—most important for every grisaille, which is a powder fine white, mixed with oils (see Chapter Nine). It takes some brain gymnastics to paint the light and leave alone what is dark. The drying is done in the mouth of a red glowing kiln. After every bit of oil has evaporated, it is fired. A second coat of paint-ing should finish the portrait.

After a mild firing, one extremely thin coat of very soft flux (Schauer #1 W or #100) is sifted over the **face only**, none over the background, at the same time the name in gold is added, and the whole fired to maturity. This coat of flux changes the evenly painted grisaille white to the texture of an old man's skin.

Beethoven Medallion

One and three-quarter inch or four and one-half centimeters high.

Of course I had to rely on portraits painted of Beethoven during his lifetime. I do not believe that he was a wild looking hater of mankind. My inspiration for this miniature came from life paintings by *Waldmüller and Torggler* (1823). The technique corresponds to the "Man's Portrait."

I immersed myself deeply into every form and line of the face and did what I could possibly do, hoping that some good spirit would guide my hand and minute brush. Whatever looks easy and natural, is really very difficult, since the slightest slip of the brush distorts the expression. Everybody who tried once, knows it.

The technique is similar to the two portraits already discussed. I had this task because there **are** situations where one depends either on photography or available contemporary art. A warning: Never try to do *portraits* with cloisonné wires: humans have no wire-sharp lines in their faces, unless they depict symbolic figures....

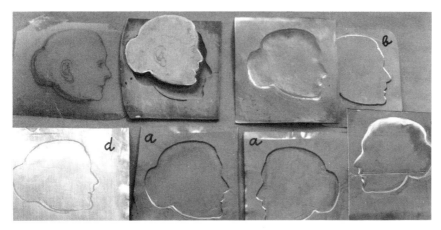

What a bonus it would be for a skillful enamelling painter if one could safely multiply portrait miniatures, each still remaining an original executed in very different techniques, and spare the preparation of the metal and the transfer of drawing and all that metalwork. So the practical department of my old mind contemplated:

Here is a way to do it. Profiles make it easier: The technique is a variation of T&D. The original is made from life, if that is possible. When transferring the design onto a metal surface, paint it with tempera white, let dry, and either with carbon paper or rubbing soft pencil over the back of the design (which should be on a thin tracing paper), put it in place on the white surface of the metal and with a sharp pencil draw over the lines. On bare copper, carbon paper alone will do—it can be cleaned off. But an enamelled surface would not be save from residues. Use 20 gauge copper for the T&D. Saw it out, stay outside of the line. Do not file, just take off the burr.

On bare copper the design may be traced first and then drawn with either Underglaze D or with ceramic pencil.

There are numerous possibilities to apply the T&D. If the portrait is to be slightly raised, use only the open part of it and pressing with fingertips (or a plastic spoon for larger areas) will do.

That worthless bit of copper is priceless in what it can do: The face is *set deep* for enamelling the head only, leaving the surrounding precious metal un-enamelled. Since profiles are the same seen from either side, the choice is up to the artist. Or enamel the background and engrave or etch the lines of the face into the precious metal, and leave it as a golden image on a colored or even very richly decorated background. Such an image should not be too small. Or, for the slightly raised face as old enamel compositions have, see what Chapter Four can tell you.

Or a minute portrait on a small thin piece of metal: Just place N-T gold, silver, or copper (0.15 millimeters is thick enough) over the opening of that T&D quite lightly, just to get a clear outline, and then flatten the thin metal again with a mallet on a flat surface, and paint.

Plan—I mean PLAN—on paper how the whole process will be executed. Portraits (miniatures) ARE a most demanding theme. However, if you can draw and find ONE line which is characteristic for a profile...more power to you!

Chapter Twenty-three
Gifts of Honor

I prefer to label these items as *gifts of honor* or *recognition* or *service awards*, because the word *trophies* always reminds me of scalps dangling from somebody's belt.

One could really make a show of monstrosities by collecting what is available to those who try to find a pleasing and tasteful award for people who are worthy of something special.

Here is a fine opportunity for enamellers and metal smiths to produce gifts which not only honor the receiver but give true pleasure. These objects are one need not be ashamed of like plastic-marble, imitation gold, or grand statues in miniature.

I have chosen a twig of laurel for most of these objects. I am showing these to you, not to be copied, but so that you can understand their construction, and make your own original piece. By the way, *Laurel* was sacred to *Apollo*, the eternally youthful Greek god. Protector not only of the arts, he was the choir director of the nine muses, the charming young females who symbolized all that gives grace to our lives. Greek gods were thoroughly human, but at the same time had eternity to get into all kinds of problems—and they did. Apollo tried to win over a young nymph. The nymph, who must have had her reasons, rejected Apollo and turned herself into a laurel tree. He could only pick a branch—**that branch**.

The Shield

If the enameller is not a good metal worker, he/she must cooperate with a silversmith, or the other way around. It is not meant to be a one-of-a-kind piece, but can be produced in unlimited numbers. The emblem shield in front is set separately, held in place with a wooden spacer. Then the roof holds all parts together and is itself fastened with a screw. In this case, a sphere of light green jade disguises the screw. The construction of the metal is explained by the following drawings and slides.

The Making of the Emblem

This enamelled emblem in the shape of a shield may depict anything befitting the purpose of the gift, from the simplest to the most intricate cloisonné. There is no limit to imagination. The back of the shield's container has plenty of space for engraving. I used copper which was gold-plated.

Several ways to enamel the emblem:

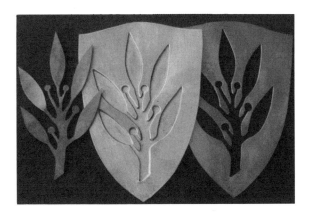

T&D provides the enameller with multiple shapes ready for enamel, without soldering.

Silver, 0.15 to 0.20 millimeters thick needs counter enamel, so does eighteen carat N-T gold. Fine gold, 0.10 to 0.15 millimeter thick, does not, except if the back is enamelled with the same care as the front and/or for a more substantial feeling. The cut out silver branch in the middle may be enamelled all over, or the negative branch only. The copper parts serve as stencils.

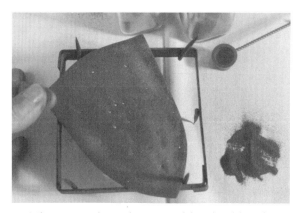

The cutout branch received hard soldered wires to fit into holes in the enamelled background.

Silver foil fired under a transparent enamel.

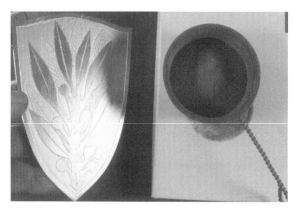

The branch is etched in differing depths into the copper and then enamelled.

Construction of the Shield

The first step for the champlevé technique used for the shield was to draw the more detailed branch on adhesive paper glued to the shield. Holes were drilled where the berries are, and with a jeweller's saw, the branch was cut out.

The open piece was turned over and soldered on a flat copper backing. Cleaned in acid and counter enamelled again, the front was wetpacked and fired, then stoned, and gold-plated.

Constructing the metal for the shield:

After the enamelling was done, the metal body of the shield had to be constructed of eighteen gauge copper. Around a wooden core of the size of the body planned, a boxlike shape is formed and soldered with silver solder, fitting not too tightly. A wooden mallet prevents distortion.

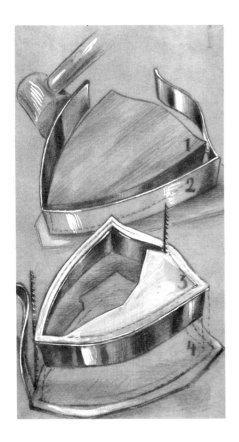

This copper frame is then soldered to a flat piece of copper, turned upside down, and the exact contours of the future frame of the enamelled shield are incised with a sharp point, adding the width of one millimeter overhang inside and outside of this line. The inside of this flat part is carefully sawn out, filed, and after protecting all solder joints with ochre, it is soldered to another flat piece of copper which is cut out identically to the open frame on top.

For the **neck** an exact model of x-ray film was made and then constructed of eighteen gauge copper sheet. It received a bottom, and the steel nut was soldered into this "neck," leaving enough space for the bolt. When you assemble it, leave enough open space so as not to touch the point of the shield's container.

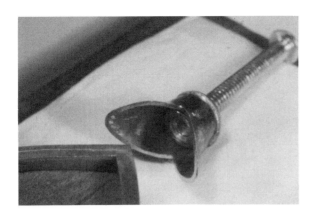

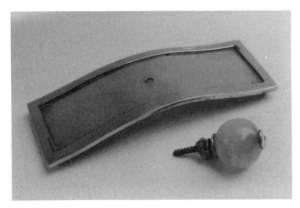

The **roof** of the shield is also formed over the wooden core; it received a flat rim all around and vertical rims on each side, which will hold the roof in place when it is finally mounted. The roof must be removable and will be held with light tension by a decorative screw. In this case it is hidden by a large bead of jade. The entire construction can be easily multiplied for any special purpose. Only the enamelled emblem is interchangeable. The shape of such a gift of honor is up to the designer.

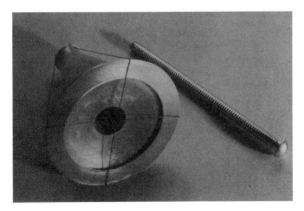

Looking at the bottom: crossed iron wires hold the parts together during hard soldering.

The **nodus** and the method how it is built has been described in earlier chapters.

After engraving whatever is desired, all parts are gold-plated and assembled, first sliding the enamel into the front, then the wooden spacer. If the fit seems a bit loose, add thin leather or cardboard, and a drop of glue helps.

All is done once the bolt is threaded through the foot and turned tightly inside the nut housing within the neck.

A point to remember: Protect the design and finished pieces legally from plagiarism!

The Medal

These use silver or gold-plated silver, tombac, or copper as a base metal. The motif is executed using cloisonné/champlevé techniques. It has a loop on its back to put it on a chain, so that it can be worn as a pendant. The metal is thick enough so that it does not have to be counter enamelled. This also makes it possible for the back to be engraved.

The Cup

A demonstration of champlevé on a round vertical copper shape.

The cup has been hand raised and is planned for enamelling on its foot and nodus. If anything ever happens to it, it can easily be taken apart, repaired, and put together again. For a special commission, precious metal work would have been chosen.

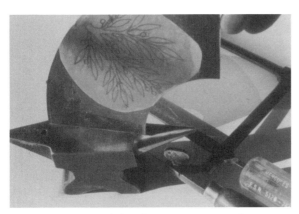

From a conical development cut out from x-ray film, the foot was sawn from eighteen gauge copper. The design is glued in place and ready to be cut out. The vertical solder joint is checked for flawless fit.

A backing of fine silver is fitted and hard soldered behind the piece cut out of the twig of laurel. **No** gaps where the solder had to flow!

The foot was rounded over a wooden stake (to avoid distortions) with a wooden mallet. Binding wire holds the seam tightly in place. Iron wire tightens in the glow of the flame while copper expands which helps.

After acid cleaning and reshaping the foot (and at the same time the small sleeve over the nut housing) the insides were coated with **Vaseline**. Plaster of Paris was poured inside, and to soak surplus water out, the foot was put on a pillow of paper tissues. When the plaster was dry and hard...

..I placed the foot between lead sheet in a vice and set the silver evenly deep with a punch.

Mixing the utterly useful reinforced ochre from old pieces of iron wire and wet ochre to a thick paste, it is fitted into the two openings—a wire sticking out to get a hold of each. These pieces are pre-fired in the kiln (after thorough drying!) and may now be used each time the enamel on the foot is inserted into the kiln. A bit of moist ochre may be added to hold the two openings in perfect shape.

Enamel is wetpacked and Scalex painted over the bare copper to avoid oxidation flakes on the enamel.

It takes two to three layers of enamel.

The enamelling is finished, the three enamelled parts are cleaned, polished, and ready to be gold-plated.

Before assembling all...

..see how the enamelled ring of the nodus is prevented from sliding.

This is the only time I use pewter solder: To hold the nut housing in the exact center of the springy-hard **cup**, which would turn soft if it were heated to a glow.

The Ring

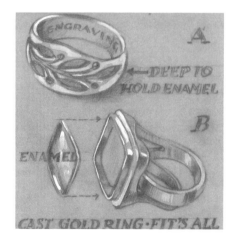

A. This ring can be cast in either gold or silver. It has enough thick material in its shank so that it may be hammered to any size. Inside, there is space for engraving.

B. This ring is made to fit any finger. It is enamelled on top, and on the inside is space for lettering.

The Paperweight

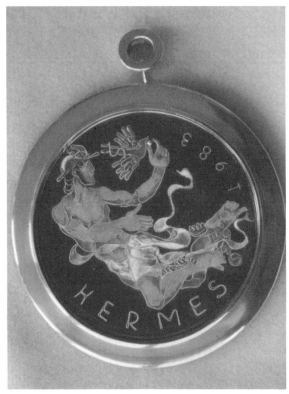

For a successful business person this could be a conversation piece on the desk or it could be hung on the wall (three-and-one-half inches in diameter). Is it some kind of modern witchcraft to know how to be remembered every day by a special person or place? Put something small, useful, good to look at, and nice to touch, and if possible, with an amusing and inspiring theme, right on the desk of that person. I suggest an object of art, of fine hand skills, under the pretense of a paperweight. Everybody needs them, but they should be of good taste and have value.

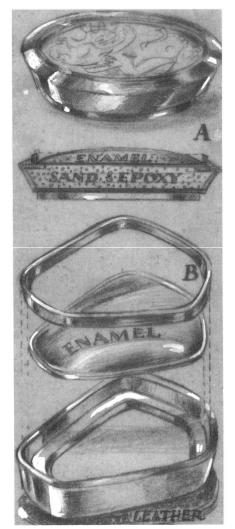

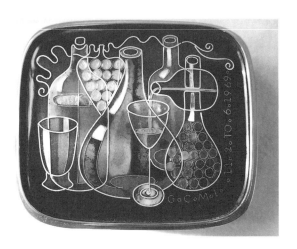

A gift for a glass producing company:
Silver cloisonné set into the cover of a pewter box.

Chapter Twenty-four
Triptych

NUM CUSTOS FRATRIS MEI SUM EGO?

Enamel on metal, both rather indestructible, became the material which forced me to express with a few inches or feet of flat wire (gold, silver, or copper), what made me tick—the pains and promises of our century. I set the images of the Bible side by side with us as contemporaries. It happened without being planned.

Technically, the three panels set into dark wood, hold no problem. The only concern was to set them theft-proof. It happened with some of my work that someone unscrewed and stole six panels from an altar cross.

The triptych **Path of Destruction.**

The left panel has Adam reaching for the calamitous fruit from the *Tree of Knowledge*, not for Eve's God-given nature. We, today, begin to know what is good and what is evil about that knowledge.

The center plaque shows man's violence and the deceptive triumph he is lead to, and the third panel is complete destruction of nature and civilization.

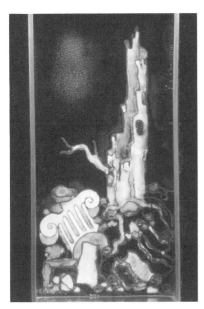

The Latin text in English is (vertical) Cain, where is your brother Abel? and (horizontal) Am I my brother's keeper? Am I?

Chapter Twenty-five
Five Panels for
Temple Emanu-El
in Wichita, Kansas

It began with the **triptych** (Chapter Twenty-four) which I had made for nobody special, but as my reaction to violence and the destructive sense-lessness of war. A group of Jewish patrons of fine art had seen it and asked me if I would and could create a piece for their new temple.

Since pictures of men or animals are not part of the sanctuary, these five panels are framed in black wood and set into the red brick wall as close as possible to the temple's entrance, therefore, in view of everybody who passes by.

It is indeed a daring enterprise to translate what moves human minds into a few handfuls of glass some yards of silver wire, and five small pieces of copper sheet, and preserve it for unlimited time. As a theme I suggested four of the bitter challenges of the Jewish people:

Noah who is identical with the prehistoric Upanishtim from the dawn of men's memories;

Job, the man who lost all but his faith...and got a second chance;

Moses, who led his people to the promised land but never reached it; and

The bitter twentieth century
Before the image of the letter *J*, standing for Jehova (God), the barbed wire broke open.

And then I was at a loss for an answer. I could not leave it at this. Discussing my question with Rabbi Miller, he had the answer: Ezekiel 37: *And I will put my spirit into these slain that they may live....*

This was how immaterial thought manifested itself and has its own life from here on—a long and wondrous way into the future.

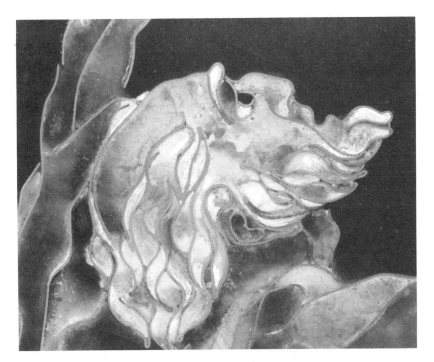

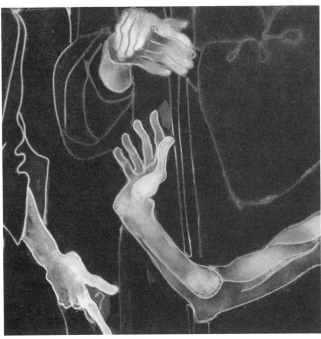

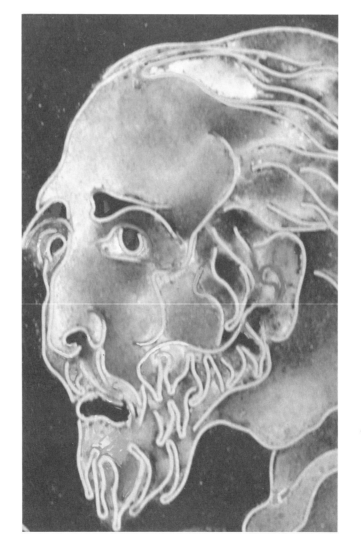

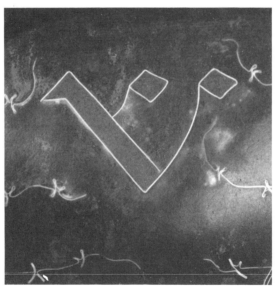

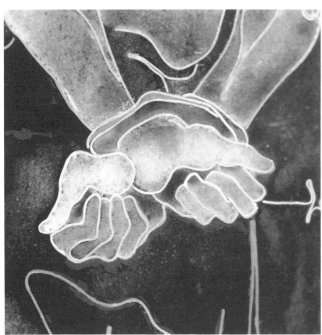

Chapter Twenty-six
Kiddush-Cup
Gold Cloisonné with
Three Sculptures

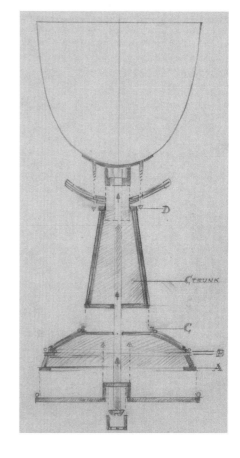

A joyous cup it is, made for a young couple who were expecting their first child. The cup is the wife's gift to her husband. It will be a family heirloom.

Let us now discuss its making and construction. The materials used are:

- N-T gold, eighteen carat.
- Sterling silver for the hand-raised cup
- Fine silver under the enamel
- Gold cloisonné wire, 0.9 millimeter high, 0.15 millimeter thick
- Pearls
- One steel bolt and nut.

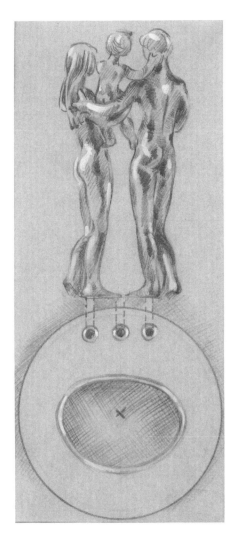

We had agreed upon design and theme: the **Tree of Life**.

The round foot had to provide space for the base of the trunk and the three golden figures. This meant an oval for the trunk, but it had to be round on top and be centered exactly above the middle of the foot.

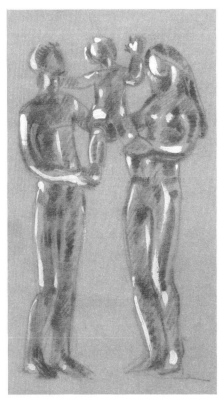

When the group of figures was made, I placed them inside a circle, drawn on paper, with the oval outline of the trunk's base.

Next, I needed a three-dimensional model of the trunk. From x-ray film I cut and glued together a conical shape close to what I imagined. X-ray film is an ideal material for such patterns: One can add with a bit of tape, one can cut away, widen, or slim it down, and make sure it provides for the vertical bolt, at exactly ninety degrees. This done, I opened the resulting pattern to a flat shape, drew a line around it on fine silver sheet, sawed it out, bent and soldered a clean-clean seam, then shaped it with a mallet over a stake.

I would need a number of fine silver rings, one millimeter thick, all differing in sizes. The sketch shows how to save silver, work, and avoid the risk of solder joints coming apart in the many firings of enamel.

The largest of these rings had to be wide enough to provide one millimeter overhang on the inside and outside of the foot's (A) vertical band for counter enamel and cloisonné lettering.

The next surrounds the slightly domed flat circle (B) on which the trunk stands. The next two are soldered to B to permit the trunk (C) to just slide in.

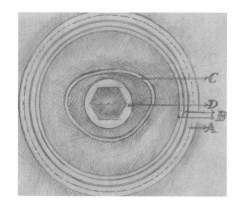

There is one part (D) left: the cover of the trunk. The drawing explains better than words. The center is cut out hectagonally and will later on admit the housing of the nut.

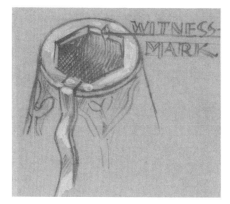

One more solution has to be found, and one more part to be constructed to assemble the hand raised (springy—hard) silver cup with the richly enamelled foot. The design for this part is free-form translation of something grown in nature. It has to hug the bottom of the cup tightly. Eight "fingers" do this better than one solid dome would. I needed the double thickness of silver and N-T gold on top cut out with spaces for enamel. It had to have eight openings to admit strong, threaded wires, which will be topped with eight round pearls floating above the idyllic composition of the young family.

They rest in eight tiny cups of solid gold. Pearls and cups are threaded and fit the eight wires which are piercing through from the silver cup.

These strong eight-threaded wires are part of a hidden silver contraption I had to invent. It is soldered with **pewter solder** (a strict **no-no** in any other case) to the bottom center of the raised cup. It holds the housing for the nut which is already in it, all hard soldered. There must be witness marks wherever they are helpful for the final assemblage.

Back to our three gold figures:

They were made separately, at the same time, and each foot had a piece of gold wire, 1/4 inch length and 1.25 millimeter thick soldered to it, and a thread cut into each. The spots where they were to penetrate the enamelled gold/ silver base are carefully marked and holes of 1.25 millimeter drilled. They can, even after enamelling, be widened if necessary. Four small square gold nuts are threaded to hold real tight when all parts are assembled. One or two more connections are needed to secure the lasting solidity of this whole artifact. A gold ribbon is added to the trunk from its **inside**, resting flat in the rim and graciously touching one spot on the trunk (with a hole for another nut and bolt) on its way elegantly covering *his* middle.

After all metal parts had been prepared, the enamelling was done. For counter enamel inside the trunk flux plus glue was swished around until all was covered. I have explained that so often that I will rush to the final assembling. The strong central bolt is inserted and screwed to the nut, this way connecting the three units.

The eight pearls are screwed into place with their gold cups; a tiny drop of glue is all right here. Pearls around the foot are held in place by tying the string with wire on four places inside the foot.

The golden family stands well up to its long future, and there is a lovely wording in gold cloisonné around the foot: **Omnia Vincit Amor**.

The golden screw cover has two holes to admit fine pliers when it is inserted. It fits tightly into the silver bottom of the assembled cup. This is the gold ribbon which stabilizes the man's figure with the trunk.

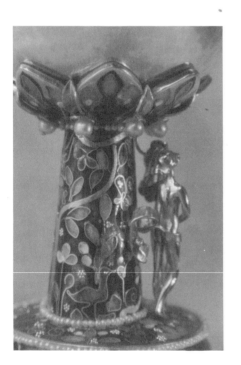

The finished cup.

Chapter Twenty-seven
The Four Seasons

This is a cloisonné enamel of eighteen inches by thirty-eight inches on a gold-colored mosaic background.

It graces the wall of a president's office, setting the tone for a pleasant first conversation, and creating a relaxed atmosphere before business even begins.

The leading idea had to be non-religious and non-political in its philosophy—something close to everybody's mind—the four seasons! Such a large composition had to be planned in small segments which fit comfortably into the kiln with all shapes interlocking like a puzzle. The many first sketches were rather small on tracing paper, one over the other, improving each line.

The four females—symbols of the seasons—came to life at first naked, and once the movements were right, I faced the old problem: What do such charming ladies wear?

Well—**Spring** is very young with birds eating out of her hands and she is clad in light white clouds and the blue of a spring sky.

Summer, womanly warm with a child on her arm, wears dark red and is surrounded by blossoming and fruit-bearing trees. Her child reaches for Spring's hands and birds.

Autumn, amidst an abundance of color and fruit baskets filled to the rim, collects apples into her wide apron, and is hardly able to hold the bounty.

And **Winter**—my winter, is timelessly young in spite of her white hair. She is pregnant with the next year's delights. Her garment is sparkling fog and icicles—**not** naturalistic ones, but slim shapes of fine silver fired under transparent light grays. A wrap of wintry dark envelops her figure and the grapevine and birds she protects. It sounds like poetry? IT IS!

The first small design was enlarged to the desired size of the final piece by photocopy. In cutting and gluing these enlargements together the final design evolved.

A second enlargement served for a rough balancing of colors which was done with watercolors.

The most practical way to retain the line drawing as a guide for bending cloisons, and to feel free to paint the entire composition with oil colors without losing the design is a *sheet of clear glass* a bit larger than the enamel panel to be. It is placed over the original drawing, which for reason of seeing mistakes easier, is reversed. All lines are marked with felt pen, again concentrating and simplifying the image. This being done, the glass is turned over again and the entire plaque is painted freely with artist's oil paint. Mistakes can easily be wiped off. The gold background is filled in, too.

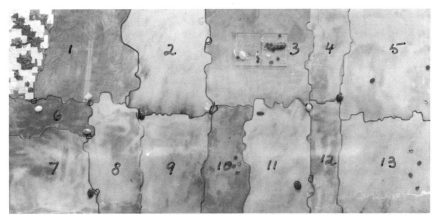

The glass is turned over again and covered with tracing paper, then the composition is divided into handy sections on the paper and together with x-ray film cut into exact patterns. These are stiff enough so that their outlines can be traced and incised on to sixteen gauge copper sheet, all being numbered. The burr from sawing is increased with a rough upward file stroke.

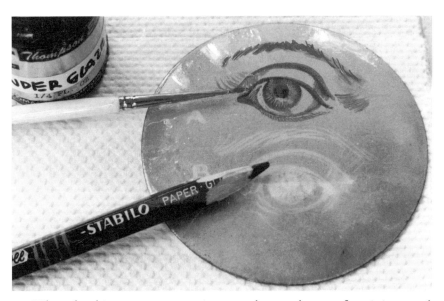

When the thirteen copper sections are clean and grease free, it is a good time to apply the line design: Tracing with red carbon paper will do. For a dark permanent, Underglaze D will do. For colorless, light lines, all Stabilo pencil is changing from black to bright under a coat of high fried flux.

Counter enamel is sifted in two to three thin layers, spraying glue after each application. A solid crust covers the back of each segment, once it is dry.

Now sift flux over the fronts, place each section on mica and fire, one after the other. If some mica sticks, that is all right.

If the design is not yet fired, it may be added now on top of the fired flux, with red carbon paper or a ceramic pencil, or with an electric engraver, which is the cleanest method.

My suggestion is to use sixteen gauge 1.2 millimeter high copper cloisonné wire. It is easier to stone clean.

The fine silver foil, laid in small rectangles, is fired at the same time the cloisons are set, but no wires are *on* the foil because they would have no hold.

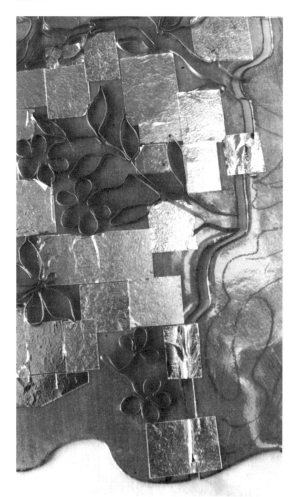

Several gold tones are mixed with transparent yellow, mauve, gray, tan, and some olive green. Samples are essential!

Wherever cloisons continue on the next section, let them stand over the rim and cut them off after they are wetpacked and fired.

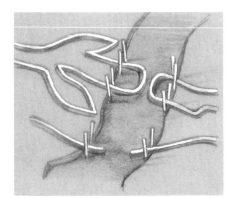

And here are a few pictures which need no words:

Chapter Twenty-eight
Altar with Five Large Cloisonné Panels

The congregation of Saint Peter's in New Hampshire entrusted me with the design of an altar and the enamels as part of it. It is always a great responsibility to think up and create what is sacred to people. A very fine cabinet maker was to cooperate with me, as the large enamels of the front not only had to sit deeply for protection, but I wished to see them in their own space—not only physically. A large leaf-gilded frame takes care of this. On top of the altar is the ancient symbol of Mary: **Amate**—love one another—also in gold leaf on a mild grey of the wood.

How is an artist crafts (wo)man to bring his/her thoughts and design convincingly to the congregation? One must learn to know, to respect, and to like each other. A small model of the altar and the five very differing expressions of Saint Peter, quite carefully but lively sketched, photographed as slides and shown almost life size to the group of members of Saint Peter's, open the eyes and say more than words alone can.

There are also the questions of price, of time of delivery, and of all of the material things to be discussed and answered in a sensible manner. Only then can the work begin.

On the left is a very human fisherman, Peter, trusting Jesus that on the other side there will be plenty of fish. Peter is even more human when he does not trust enough to be able to walk on water, and he would have drowned if Jesus had not pulled him up. The center panel stands as a symbol of that *Rock of a Man*. The fourth panel: betrayal and despair. The naive young woman's hand seems to say: "But you know him you were with him!" The last of the five panels symbolizes the changed man Peter, who is willing to love and care for mankind which Saint John's gospel call Jesus' sheep.

  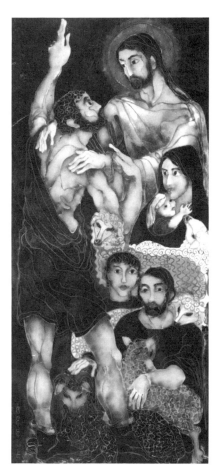

When I laid out the work to be done, the interior size of my kiln limited me to eight-by-eight-inch panels. Two of these fitted together in lines of wires and the colors had to match. An eight inch by eight inch panel of eighteen gauge copper is quite heavy when several coats of enamel are applied on both sides, and if any minor catastrophe during work should happen, such a panel could be repeated. It is already quite large for a piece of cloisonné, which has to be controlled inch by inch, stoned later on, and kept flat. Chapter Seven holds all the information about the technique of cloisonné.

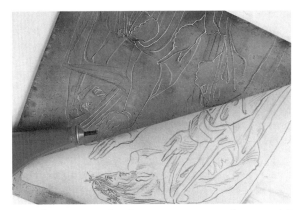

After tracing the design on copper, the traced lines are engraved with an electric hand tool. The residue of carbon paper and grease can be washed off, leaving the copper immaculate and the design permanent.

During the many firings, it might happen that some wires do not connect too well with the neighboring panel. Or one discovers too late that a wire is simply wrong—it has to be pulled out, or ground out, with a small diamond impregnated wheel, like dentists use.

LORD, I AM SPENT BY
THE BLOWS OF
THY HAND
SURELY
EVERY MAN
IS A
MERE
BREATH

PSALM 39

SPIRITUS·EST

QUI·VIVIFICAT

CARO·NON·PRODEST·QUIDQUAM·

THE CUP OF '88

by Margarete Seeler

The theme of the lower part of this cup
is the fears and problems which haunt
us all: the misuse of science for destruction;
the breakdown of human relations. The
upper part of the cup tries to raise hope, trust,
healing and healthy thinking. Again, I have
found it best to make this statement with figures
from the Bible, to say what is really almost impossible to address universally. You see St.
Michael, and underneath him, the atom bomb
and some of its victims. Also, two of the symbols
which seem to run the world: the dollar sign
and the atom. On the other side of the cup is
a human couple with their child...all is right
and full of life; while on the foot sits that
evil creature, maybe death itself, holding
reign to the chains of man like an animal
of burden; the dollar sign above the
whole unpleasant and too-true scene.

*Fig. 1. "The Cup of '88", the other front -
Genesis 1.26/28, "and multiply".*

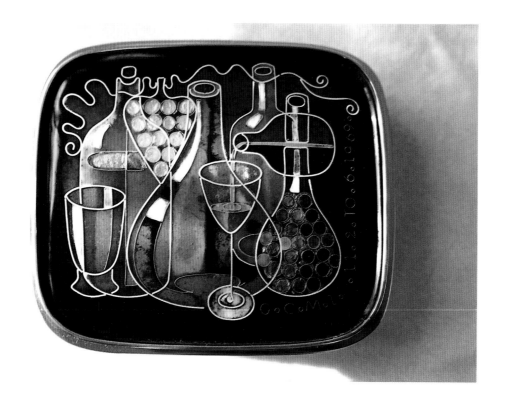

The illustration shows how to cut a slim groove into the enamel, down to the copper, and along the correct new line. I set a new wire into this channel, packed it tightly with enamel plus Klyr-Fire and went on working over the whole plaque. The moment it is fired and still red hot, I put some pressure on the corrected wire with a hot spatula. Not much of a problem.

If the counter enamel on the backs needed some new coats, then Klyr-Fire and one or two thin coats of enamel sifted form a crust—glue is the last! When it was really dry, I turned it upside-down, placed it on the **mica**-covered wire-mesh trivet and continued work on the front. The new counter enamel melted into the old and bits of **mica** are stuck—so what!

As long as the copper cloisons are not imbedded or at least covered with enamel, they oxidize after each firing and need cleaning in acid or Sparex. All traces of oxidation being removed, the plaque was then sponged over with ammonia and scrubbed with a glass brush under running water before wetpacking the next layer of enamel colors.

The drawing on page 285 shows a flat piece of steel with a handle which is kept hot on top of the kiln. Size about eight inch by eight inch. The moment when I took the glowing plaque out of the kiln and set it on top of the kiln (trivet, mica and panel) this steel square was placed onto it, forcing it to remain and cool **flat**. Since I worked with two sets of trivet and mica, I continued with the enamelling. Whenever one plaque is wetpacked, all moisture is soaked out with tissue paper or clean old linen, and when it is completely dry—like sand on the beach—I tap it as even as possible with the tip of a finger and brush off what is too much.

DO STOP when you are tired. When concentration fades, silly mistakes happen which are hard to undo.

Well—the moment comes when all seems to be done and one is ready for stoning. **What a job** that is on ten times eight inches by eight inches. To confess, such large surfaces cannot really be done by hand, except for faces, hands, and some especially delicate areas, and for the final finish. I used an electric belt sander with waterproof, finest grid sandpaper until all wires were *out*, which means visible without enamel on top. Then I went on by hand. Some low spots remained and were filled with just enough clear flux for light hues and transparents for darker areas. And I fired one more time. The panels were now glossy again and that is what the images of saints and their kind should not be. They need the understated **matte**. To stone all over again is dangerous for the colors and a torture to the artist. I used a glass etching chemical. (Hydrofluoric acid if you can get it, and if you can work outside with a mask before your nose and mouth, and protective glasses for the eyes.) The matting done, neutralize with ammonia, glass brush under running water, dry the panels, and rub in the finest cabinet maker's paste wax you can get. Polish with a warm hand.

After all ten panels were completed, they were to be attached to a large wooden board, fitting exactly under the already leaf-gilded framing.

At the cabinet maker's shop we put quite a heavy layer of an elastic two component epoxy over a hard board, then covered it with a kind of thin burlap, added another layer of epoxy on top, and placed the ten panels with utter care onto this still soft bed of hardening epoxy. In this manner we could improve on the evenness and the connections and check their places inside the golden framework. This being done, the capable hands of the cabinet maker did the rest.

The congregation of Saint Peter's knows *their* altar like one knows one's best friend and we hope that the symbols, standing for important thoughts, will have much to say, to answer, and to console.

The altar is finished, and the five panels are set into a leaf-gilded wooden frame.

Chapter Twenty-Nine
Enamel Combined with Pewter

Today's pewter[1] is a bright, silver-colored, non-tarnishing, and rather soft metal. It is an alloy of tin, antimony, bismuth, and copper—**no lead**. It is pleasant to the touch and its neutral color makes it ideal to hold or frame enamels, especially in combination with wood. It is rather easy to shape with a few tools, as no hot torches are needed, just a tiny flame from a handheld propane bottle. It comes as sheet and wire of differing thicknesses. All this might encourage enamellers to learn the use of it.

[1]Pewter melts at a very low degree (425 degrees to 440 degrees Fahrenheit) and must never enter a kiln.

Producing the cross and the two candlesticks affords almost all the know-how one would need for boxes, frames, hollow ware, and the setting of enamels. The themes of the silver cloisonné plaques: In the center are grapes and wheat, symbolizing bread and wine and the host. To the left and right are the Alpha and Omega reaching from the very beginning beyond the end. At the foot is the snake, the earthly and material temptation, and at the head of the cross the symbol for the immaterial holy spirit—the dove.

The height of the cross is approximately eighteen inches (forty-eight centimeters).

The thickness of the pewter is sixteen gauge and fourteen gauge.

Of course, a correct design was done before any metal work could be started, and the enamels, according to the plan, were made and finished.

While working on these three pieces, I made photographs and wrote the captions to go with each. They explain exactly how to approach such a task:

The finished candlestick.

A conical development of the pewter cone was drawn and a pattern of it cut from x-ray film then traced onto pewter and bent over a wooden tool, and we arrived at the rough shape the foot of the candlestick would have. To fit a flawless seam of its sides and solder it with *hard* pewter solder was the task.

The outline of the enamel plus 1/8 inch around it has been cut out. A line shows where the bezel has to be to hold the enamel.

Bezel, enamel, and the cut out are fitted and properly soldered (medium hard solder).

A strip of 1/4 inch wide pewter is soldered along the inside of the opening, 1/16 inches sticking out in front, to hold the solder in place. The heat of a tiny flame is used from the inside of the cone, which makes the solder flow on both sides.

Another strip of pewter has been soldered around the insert, for safe and easy assembling.

A wide framing is added outside the opening, all is filed, and polished, and ready to be put together. The enamel is covered with...

...several layers of tape for protection.

When adding to the upper bowl of the nodus and the enamelled ring around it, the even heights have to be checked again and again.

As has been explained before, inside the cone is what is necessary for nut and bolt, which hold the candlestick parts safely together and make it possible to take it apart, if any repairs should be needed.

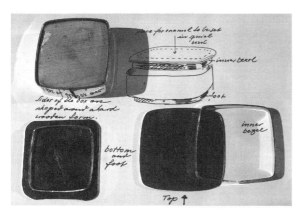

Boxlike shapes for the arms of the cross, the slightly larger center and the in between parts are shaped and mounted over wooden...

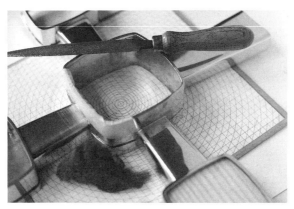

...spacers, which remain inside the cross. Only wooden tools are used, since metal would widen the soft metal.

After all metal work has been done, only the wooden parts inside the cross are set into their exact place. They are held by tape and wedges. After all enamels are mounted, the channel for the steel rod to be inserted is drilled.

The sketch explains how the enamels, on their spacers, are safely placed and held.

The same is done on the back of the cross: Pewter on top of the wood, rims soldered around each. Only the cover in the center has the etched-in ancient symbol: **Amate**.

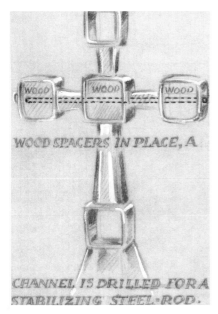

WOOD SPACERS IN PLACE, A

CHANNEL IS DRILLED FOR A STABILIZING STEEL-ROD.

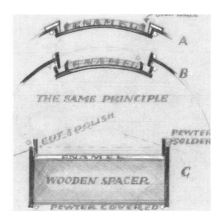

THE SAME PRINCIPLE

WOODEN SPACER.

PEWTER COVERED.

After all is accomplished, the steel rod is inserted. Its entry and exit are closed with small pewter disks soldered with easy-flow pewter solder, filed, and polished.

Eight and one-half foot tall *wooden cross* with inlaid pewter lines and an enamelled twenty-two inch diameter silver cloisonné, the symbol enamelled over fine silver. Set into a wide pewter frame.

The last soldering with pewter solder is done on the finished cross and the wood is protected with asbestos sheet. The inlaid strips of pewter are safely placed between wood. Only the solder joint remains exposed. Design and enamel by Seeler. Pewter by Felten. Wood by Lundy.

The frame around the gold closionné plaques is pewter (see "Book of Gospels," Chapter Nineteen).

Gold grain enamel, set into the handle of a pewter box.

Hectagonal pewter box by Hans Zeitner (20.5 centimeters in diameter = 8 1/8 inch) holding a limoges enamel by Seeler, centered with a cabochon emerald.

Pewter box with T&D cloisonné in the handle by Joanne Conant.

Hangers for enamels, set into
wood, front and back.

Pewter boxes with enamel.

Chapter Thirty
Enamel in Combination with Ebony, Ivory, Wrought-iron, Weaving, Wood, and Polished Stone Surfaces

Enamelling as an end in itself has come into being only in this century. In earlier times enamels were always a part of artifacts in every size, from the enormous Far Eastern vases and figures to tiny miniatures to be held or hidden in a gold ring or locket. Here we are right in the middle of the unlimited possibilities: Enamel set between two thin sheets of ebony and/or ivory.

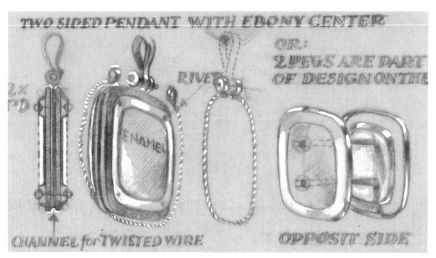

Eighteen carat gold cloisonné held between wood of quite large size. Chapter Fifteen describes this eighteen-carat N-T gold panel *Unisono*. To give it the right framing and to accentuate its colors, I chose a very neutral gray stain for the wood, and set the enamel into a step-up wooden frame, inlaid with a line of polished brass. The hanger echoes the theme of the panel and is a jewel in itself. The receptacle for the wall hook is hidden beneath the hollow amethyst.

A large cloisonné plaque is set deep into wood and is framed and held in place with a rectangular frame of pewter, the vertical part is tightly adjusted to the minimal irregularities of the enamel. The wood will be stained black and waxed.

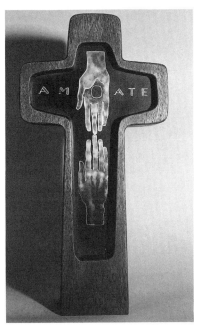

The cross is walnut, a block tapered from its bottom square to a rectangle. A slice of approximately one-half inch (1.2 centimeter) thickness, also diminishing towards the top, was sawn off. The window, a bit smaller than the enamel, was cut out, and all edges rounded. After inserting the silver cloisonné (set deep into the wooden block), the wood was glued together again. Enamel and cross are waxed over a perfect finish (opaque enamel over darkest transparent gray).

To enhance and protect enamelled bowls, rims of pewter are covering the lips. Before sifting any enamel, a copper rim about one inch tall was soldered to the bottoms of the spun copper. After the enamel was fired, this foot, which received no enamel, got a sleeve plus bottom of pewter. Although they were easy to fit and set, a screw underneath the stone of the blue bowl shows how to add solidity. Any irregular-shaped enamelled container also will win in value by this combination.

Two silver cloisonné plaques four-and-one-half inches (11.5 centimeters), are set into a wide pewter rim with a wooden spacer between the enamels. Photographed with a mirror to see both sides. The first idea to set them was on top of a handwrought iron candelabra.

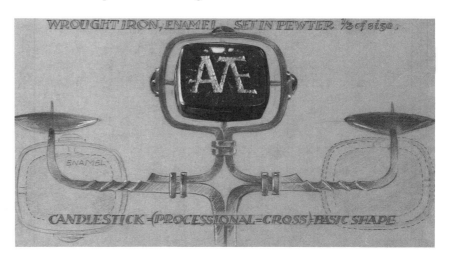

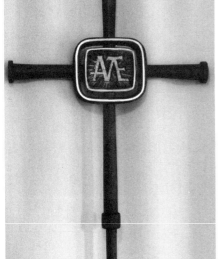

The plan was changed to a wooden processional cross. Both enamels are cloisonné partly fired over silver and gold foil.

An ancient bible, bound in re-used, even older parchment, is safely housed in a walnut box; on the inside cover is an enamel with the name of the owner. On the cover of the closed box a cross-shaped enamel is set with a biblical quotation.

One more interesting duo: Large woven tapestries and enamelled shapes become partners in a tree of life.

Gold-plated cloisonné sits deep in semi-precious stone slabs, or marble.
The deep part is ground out with diamond-impregnated and sanding-linen wheels. They may be set in metal bezels and held with nuts and bolts from the (leather-covered) back.

Chapter Thirty-one
Pearls and Semi-precious Stones Combined with Enamel

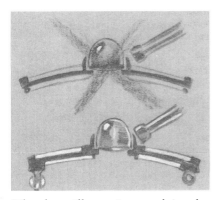 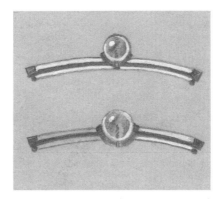 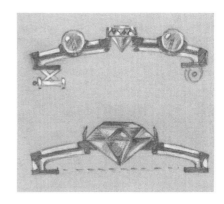

The above illustrations explain why stones and pearls must be set on a metal island to protect the enamelled areas from pressure while bezels are closed, or holes drilled.

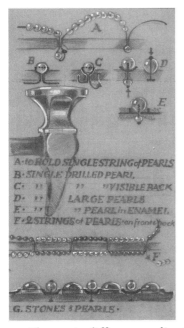

Shows six different applications of pearls.

The underside of a cup receives a string of seed pearls in sections, which are held tightly by wire loops from the (invisible) inside, and are threaded through small holes.

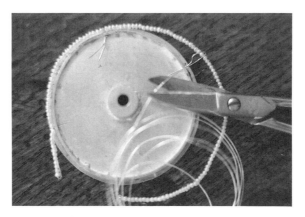

Since the T&D method has been explained in Chapter Three, this sketch goes a big step ahead:

A combines the T&D made bezel top, the enamel underneath rests on ivory or ebony (or a drilled stone); and it shows how these three layers are stitched together. A drop of jeweller's glue is useful.

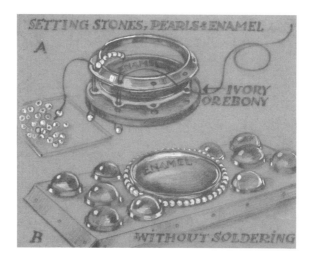

B The enamel in a round bezel (T&D) rests on wood or hard board, and so do the ten cabochon stones. The rectangular metal with the open bezels covers all. This metal shape is produced and reproduced as many times as needed, be it as sides for a precious box (see Chapter Eleven) or as long partitions (see page 87, the "Verdun Altar").

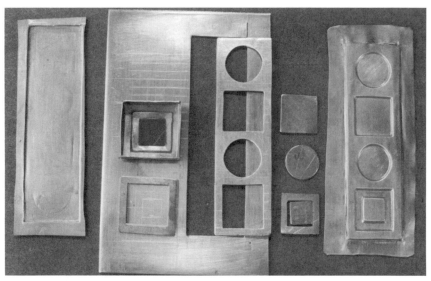

Enamellers who had no chance to learn gold smithing face a problem if they wish to combine and include stones with their work in a good craftsman's quality. May I share with you a method I have found: It is again built on the T&D technique using one millimeter eighteen gauge thick copper sheet for the T&D and 0.5 millimeter (twenty-two gauge) thick metal for the imprints to be enamelled.

For rectangular frames, a T&D corner. It provides box-like settings for round or square stones. (You go on to new shapes from here!)

The centers are cut out, and over square or round mandrels the bezels are sharpened.

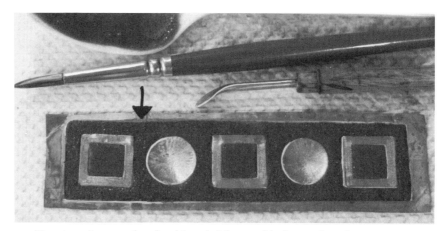

Two imprints are hard soldered (silver solder), overlapping...
...or in a rectangle.

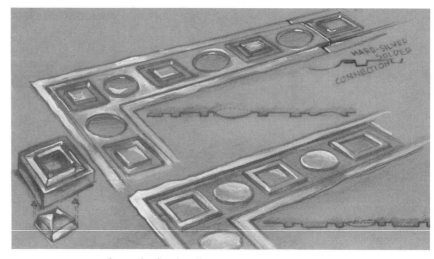

Stones are set from the back, all parts are mounted on a wooden or metal surface.

Back to the combination of pearls and enamel. Metal: N-T gold, T&D technique.

Two muses playing music—gold cloisonné set onto ivory. The illustration on page 262 tells about the strand of pearls which sits on the gold rim of the enamel.

  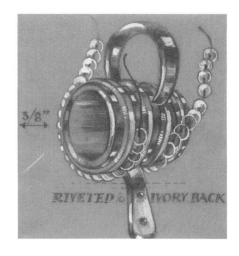

Let us discuss the small cylinder through which the chain runs: Four wire rings are soldered around it. Pearls are placed between the outer ones. In the center space a forged gold loop connects the hanger to the back ivory.

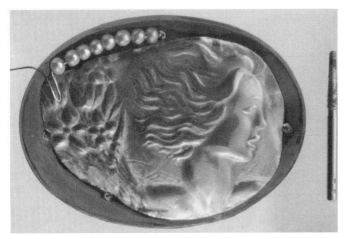

The oval of flat jade is one-and-one-half inches (3.75 centimeters) wide and three-eighths inch (0.5 centimeters) thick. The gold relief is solidly backed with a two-component epoxy, which could be filed flat. Around the gold I drilled small holes (add a drop of water), to receive the wire onto which small pearls are strung. Underneath the relief are the necessary holes drilled to fasten the findings. The drill used is diamond-impregnated.

The cloisonné and T&D brooch you saw started under Chapter Three receives a double rim of pearls.

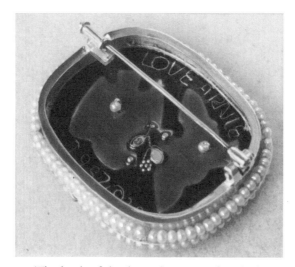

The back of this brooch is treated with the same care as the front. Inside of two round cloisons it has indentations and holes provides to hold two larger pearls on front, tied with thin gold wire to two tiny pearls on the back. A minute drop of jeweller's instant glue is added.

Chapter Thirty-two
About Design

Designing is as personal an activity as is handwriting. To the untaught Navajo woman who made this enamel without needing any instruction, no problem existed, neither in bending the wires nor in choosing those strong colors. The simple motif is part of her nature, and of her being, part of an ancient culture.

White peoples' tastes are too influenced by the many styles of the past, and especially by the super sweetness of the nineteenth and early twentieth centuries.

The suggestions I put on this paper are my very own ways to approach design: I look at nature. Not only at the very outer appearance, but I try to understand what inner law of life and development made this form. How does life itself and growth happen in a tree, a twig, a flower, a crystal, a human body, a human eye, or hand? To catch this spark of life is not just skill anymore but reaches into the domain of **art**. One cannot force it—one must almost become part of the object.

This is a painting with grisaille white direct from a drawing after nature.

This same **iris** study was translated into very freely bent wires, a true translation into enamel (glass and metal). But I had to know every square inch of my iris, otherwise something quite nonsensical would have resulted.

A nature motif. Geometrically repeated, it is a good solution for a hollow nodus, or a flat pattern to sift enamel over—a beginning for numerous possibilities.

Figure studies, drawing as close to nature as is needed for an idealization of the mythical three graces, so they became **ideas** again (not nice little nudes).

Or the translation into expressive cloisonné wires of a man in despair (from Book Cover, Chapter Nineteen).

This is a small sample detail of five large drawings rich with human figures. They were the start for the five panels of the altar front (Chapter Twenty-Eight). They are the personifications of mutual joy, of lack of trust, trustworthiness, and betrayal.

After the basic design on paper was done (on scraps of paper, details glued together, the translation into simplifying wires and enamels happened almost by itself.

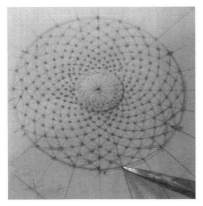
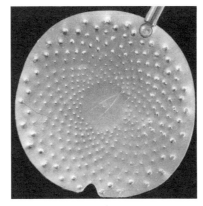

Inspired by nature's often repeated design, almost abstract in its geometrical order!

On the small piece of thin gold it is set deep with punches of different sizes and might become gold granulation or gold grain enamel in a brilliant transparent.

Chapter Thirty-Three
Hints from A - Z

Acids

Always add acid to water, never water to acid.

Nitric Acid

is used for cleaning gold, to enhance its color, and for etching copper and silver. Nitric acid does harm silver and copper, so never immerse either metal, nor anything soldered with silver solder. A few drops added to water when enamels are washed cleans the colors and removes impurities.

Sulfuric Acid

is pickle for cleaning gold, silver, copper, or guilder's metal. Never permit any iron to get into this pickle; use copper tongs to remove pieces from the acid bath. No binding wire should be left on objects to be pickled. If that does happen, silver and gold will turn copper colored. This is very hard to remove. You have to make new pickle.

Hydrofluoric Acid

is the most dangerous of acids, and must be stored either in a lead, rubber, or special plastic bottle. It destroys glass and enamel, and causes bad burns on the skin. The fumes are poisonous and the jar into which objects are immersed should have a cover and be made of acid-resistant plastic. Even so, I coat the inside and the cover with wax. (Heat the wax in a double-boiler and slosh the liquid wax around in the bowl.) A white layer of dissolved glass appears where the acid has worked; this should be wiped off with a feather or a cotton swab.

Adding Enamel Around Rims

To add enamel around rims either sift plenty over glue or salt enamel held between two fingers along the rim.

Annealing

The metal is heated to glow and immediately quenched in cold water. It becomes soft and pliable.

Asphaltum

is used to protect a surface from acid. It can be removed with lighter fuel or turpentine.

Clear, Protective Coats

consist of soft, glass-clear enamels, not too finely ground. First coat is sifted and fired only to orange peel. Second coat is added and fired fast and high.

Cloisonné Wires

How to Make Them

To buy a special size and thickness is almost impossible in the limited length we need. Buy your gold as sheet. If a rolling mill is in reach, buy one-half millimeter thickness and roll what you need. Wire 0.8 millimeter high and 0.06 thick (this is very thin like the finest Byzantine work) is excellent. Roll the gold sheet to 0.06 millimeters and cut with good small scissors whatever you need. I recommend inscribing the gold sheet with parallel lines to avoid irregular strips. You can make any size without waste and high price.

Cloisonné Wires Fall Off

when they are set directly on foil. They need a thin coat of fired enamel to melt in.

Conical Development

is the method to attain a flat pattern for a metal cone.

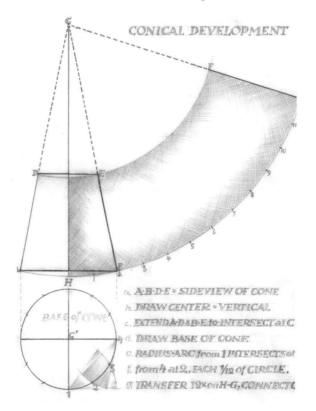

CONICAL DEVELOPMENT

a. A·B·D·E = SIDEVIEW OF CONE
b. DRAW CENTER = VERTICAL.
c. EXTEND A·D & B·E to INTERSECT at C
d. DRAW BASE OF CONE.
e. RADIUS·ARC from 1 INTERSECTS at
f. from 4 at 2, EACH 1/12 of CIRCLE.
g. TRANSFER 12×on H·G, CONNECT C

Cracking of Enamel Over a Curved Surface

Why does the enamel crack over a curved surface? Probably no or not enough counter enamel was used. Or a cloisonné wire does not quite touch the rim or the neighboring wire. The distance is either too small or not wide enough to secure the adherence of enamel. Tensions happen.

With a small diamond-impregnated tool in a flex shaft, grind along the crack and take out what is not adhering safely. Then insert either another piece of wire, touching where it must, or lay into freshly wetpacked enamel tiny silver granules, or invent an ornament which follows the rules. Sometimes enamel cracks because a rim on the back is not carefully filled. Fill it, and fire.

Degrees of Hardness of Enamels

Soft Enamels

melt at about 1300 to 1360 degrees Fahrenheit (704 to 738 degrees Centigrade). They are used on metals which cannot stand high temperatures (sterling silver) or to fill indentations at final firing when the piece should not be exposed to great heat.

Medium Enamels

melt at about 1360 to 1420 degrees Fahrenheit (738 to 771 degrees Centigrade). Most of our enamels are medium hard. If you use care and keep an eye on the work, they will be very satisfactory on sterling silver, fine silver, gold, and copper.

Hard Enamels

melt between 1420 to 1510 degrees Fahrenheit (772 to 821 degrees Centigrade). Their melting point is close to that of silver. Therefore, they should be used only on high-carat gold or copper, or in work combining both. Avoid firing hard enamels over softer ones. They will not fuse with the layers beneath and will chip and flake off.

Designing

Idea sketches, drawings, and final design are best made on tracing paper. When looked at from the other side, mistakes become obvious. Chosen sketches are enlarged via photocopying to the desired size, and corrected.

Drilling Beads or Pearls

The drill is, indeed, the successor of stone age fire drills: excellent, precise, and keeps one hand free. Bits can be sharpened on an oilstone. A bent strip of brass, drilled for different sizes of pearls, has a strong tension to hold the pearls and the fourteen gauge metal provides minute drilled cups to place the pearls.

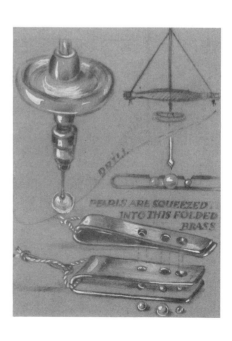

A homemade contraption to allow wire setting and wetpacking enamel around a large cup without contacting any surface.

Filing and Finishing Metal Around an Enamel

When filing and metal finishing around enamels, put layers of tape over the enamel.

Filling and Stabilizing

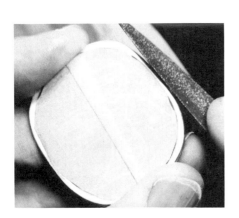

To fill and stabilize a thin gold relief against distortion, fill with a two-component epoxy, if not enamelled, and file it flat. If enamelled, fill with enamel plus binder, cover with mica, turn over, and fire both sides at the same time.

Filling Deep Areas

Before the last firing: Over light colors fill with very soft clear flux, over dark areas use light transparents of the same color.

Finger Rings

Enamelling finger rings is really asking for trouble. If it cannot be avoided, remember: Enamel must not be exposed to damage on outside domed areas and between fingers. The area should be small, deep set, or so well-protected by metal that it cannot be hit or worn off.

Construction of a Ring

a) Is the pattern and construction of a ring to be enamelled which has blue enamel under a diamond. Safe!

b) Is the bishops ring

c) An incurvature protects the counter enamelled monogram. Safe if handled with care.

d) A heavy cast ring. No counter enamel. The twig of laurel is protected.

Fitting Cover for an Enamelled Box

To have a perfectly fitting lid over any free-form shaped box provide plenty of width of the horizontal wide rim on the box's upper opening. One can always take off, but never add!

Flattening an Already Enamelled Plaque

When only one coat of flux has been fired, a plaque can still be easily flattened with strokes of the fist on a flat, hard surface or with a wooden mallet. This mallet should have leather tied over its face to soften the strokes.

One can even CUT such enamelled metal with metal scissors.

Footprints

(see Chapter Fifteen)

We discussed the three-dimensional effect under a perfectly even surface before. They were not painted but, indeed, are the imprints of four sizes of tiny feet made from pewter walking through the sand of a mix of opaques then fired just enough to retain the impression. Then filled with transparent shadow. Again barely fired, finally tightly packed with soft flux, and fired fast and hot. This is a hint, indeed, what enamel can do.

Frames

The four sides of a large enamelled panel were bent down to a box shape and were connected with its wooden frame by four screws. These sit inside the pewter bezels and are covered with four lapis lazuli. Lower left: Inside explains the simple construction.

A T&D made enamelled frame covers the screws which hold the gold cloisonné to the slab of black wood (Chapter Fifteen).

Gold

Fine Gold

is pure gold (twenty-four carat). It is the metal for exquisite enamelling. The color is different from that of eighteen-carat non-tarnishing gold. Fine gold is more yellow, while N-T gold is greenish.

N-T Gold

Eighteen-carat non-tarnishing gold (N-T gold) is an alloy of 750 parts fine gold and 250 parts fine silver, no zinc. Both metals are ideal for enamelling.

Gold-plating

Mercury gilding is not done commercially any more, except perhaps to repair an ancient piece. It is extremely dangerous. I described it in *The Art of Enamelling*, page 78. Today's professional gold-platers add a coat of nickel (or copper) first and then do the plating; this causes a difference in height on the plated object. I rather insist on having only one generous coat of gold electroplated on my pieces.

Gold-plating Copper Cloisonné

The wires must be set directly on the copper for contact. Sift flux on top, holding the piece slanted to reach the inside of each cell.

Grinding Your Own Lumps of Enamel

The mortar must be hard porcelain and the pestle must have a wooden handle. Glass or porcelain will crack. Enamel in lumps lasts for many years. Freshly ground transparents are clearer and spotless. Opaques are less sensitive.

Grisaille

Oils for Grisaille and Painted Enamel

Copaiba oil as thinner spreads soft and wide.

Turpentine as thinner gives sharp lines.

Oil of cloves and oil of lavender flows just right, and can be (after drying) taken off in the manner of a negative design and sharpened around the outsides with a wooden or plastic point.

The Perfect Surface

The enamelled background of a small and precious grisaille should have the perfection of an optical lens.

To achieve this, fire two or three thin layers of immaculately clean transparent over the metal. Then stone the surface with the same care you would take with gold cloisonné and brush under running water until no impurity is left.

Then rest the piece upside down on the trivet. Of course, the plaque should have a metal rim which touches the metal of the trivet and prevents the enamel from getting stuck to the trivet or from showing marks.

Fire fast and high—you will enjoy the result! (The same method applies to fine cloisonnés which are flash-fired).

The finest finish of cloisonné is to treat it like a precious stone on a lapidary wheel.

If grisaille is used on larger pieces, two clean layers of enamel for the background, sifted very carefully, are sufficient. The strokes of the brush should have the ease of Japanese painting. A little more pressure will spread the hair of the sable brush and widen the painted line to a shape. A small drop of color will flow and blend into such a shape quite naturally if the artist knows how to apply the technique. Try it.

Lettering

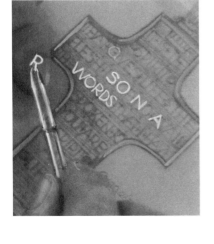

Lettering can be an important part of a piece of cloisonné enamel. It can even be made into the ornament. Here is a suggestion for bending wires to form the letters of the alphabet: Start at the point and pinch the wire to single lines (indicated by the double lines in the sketches). Except for the *X*, all the letters are bent from one piece of wire. It is advisable to trim the *I* a little for safer standing, as shown in the sketch.

Painting Colors

Enamel Painting Colors

are finely ground; they are prepared for work similar to grisaille and are dried and fired in the same manner. If you are a painter, you will find some very exciting applications of these colors as sharp line designs between areas of transparents or opaque enamel.

Fine Gold and Fine Silver Painted

as finishing touches over grisaille enamel: This technique should be used with restraint. The gold is known to the refiner as *sponge* and to the china-painter as *Roman gold*. It is ground extremely fine, then mixed like grisaille with thick oil of turpentine. The application has to be quite thick. Fire until glowing dark red or barely glowing then remove the piece and check to see if a pointed tool can still remove the gold or silver. It must adhere to the enamel. If so, polish the piece with a burnisher, or it can remain matte if treated with a glass brush under running water.

Pin

A pin stem which will not damage very fine fabric—the hinge is made of tubing. Solder another small piece of tubing in an angle of 90 degrees to the moving middle section of the hinge. Then hard solder a sewing needle (without the eye) into this second piece of tubing and attach a small ball underneath this piece to provide elasticity later on. The pin mechanic should sit high enough in order for the brooch not to hang lopsided.

Protecting Finished Enamels

during filing or polishing metal parts: Cover the enamel with two or three layers of masking tape.

Repairing Enamels

Your own: Go through the whole procedure again after you found out the reason for the damage. If a piece cannot be repaired in this professional manner, use one of the following:

Never put a piece you have not made into the kiln. Cold enamels as the market offers them are always wrong in color—maybe a black will do. It is better to mix your own. For opaque colors mix a small amount of epoxy (hard drying!) with finely ground enamel and work it into the cleaned cells or spaces with a small spatula (dentist tool). It might need another filling when dried. Cut it even with a very sharp blade and rub wax over it, if the enamel is to be half-matte. If it is to be glossy, a drop of hard, clear lacquer (like used on boats) will do. If the enamel is to be transparent, clean the damaged area thoroughly and mix the right hue from artist's oil paints with hard-drying epoxy. After drying cover with waterproof lacquer.

Minute cracks can be made almost invisible with *Walrat Spermacetti*. It is a very fine wax-like substance which hides hairline cracks in an enamelled surface. Warm the defective piece in warm water, rub minute flakes of walrat over it which will melt, and leave it for a while in a warm place. With the palm of a warm hand rub it off.

If you discover too late that a wire already fired into a cloisonné panel is wrong in design then it is ground out, down to the fluxed metal. A diamond-impregnated wheel, like dentists use, will dig a deep channel where the new wire should be. It is bent and glued into place, held by enamel which is as close as possible to the area's hues, and tightly packed with glue on top, the piece is fired—not overfired—just to hold the wire which, still glowing, is pressed into place with a slim spatula. Continue with the work; it will blend in perfectly.

Samples

If a small sample is needed of one or more colors on any metal, cut a strip one inch by one-half inch. Add the enamel(s) and melt, holding the strips in a pair of tweezers over a soldering flame. It takes only a minute and provides the information, but will crack off.

Soldering

Solder Seams

Even the cleanest solder seams show after many firings and should be hidden under a bit of design if transparent enamel has been used over the seam.

To Avoid Melting Solder

To avoid melting solder (A) running over spaces to be enamelled, file the metal edge off, (B + C) and place the solder opposite to where enamel will be. There it can be filed away.

A small bridge fixed with wire holds the two ends of a large circle of metal safely together during soldering.

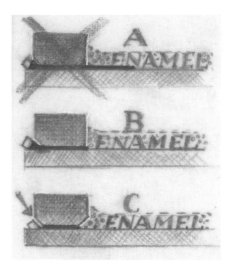

Stiffening Thin Precious Metal

To enliven and stiffen thin precious metal, punch small ornaments into the surface: Points, circles, leaves, any shape you can file from a bronze rod. Set them in a mathematical order. Both sides of, for instance, 0.15 millimeters thick gold or silver will look attractive. Use very clean transparents over front and back.

Transferring Design

Transfer Design on Bare Metal

1) Use carbon paper for the transfer and then scratch the design into the metal with a sharp point or use an electric engraver. Clean off all traces of carbon paper. Enamel over it.
2) Paint with tempera white, engrave, and wash clean.
3) Paint on bare copper with Underglaze D.
4) On enamelled surfaces: Draw with ceramic pencil on an evenly stoned surface.
5) Mark only strategic points with a diamond impregnated dental tool in a flexible shaft.

Transferring a Raised Design

(Like cloisonné wires not yet filled, or a wood cut or a leaf to an enamelled perfect surface for multiplication)

1) Remove all traces of grease, powder with talcum, and blow it off.
2) Spread squeegy oil over a glass slab and go with a clean rubber roller over the model, but not too generously.
3) Roll over the design to be transferred.
4) Wax paper is tightly placed, shiny side down, over the oiled design and left there for a few minutes. Remove the wax paper and
5) Place it on the enamelled surface; oily shiny side down—it must touch everywhere.

6) Remove the wax paper and sift powder—fine ground enamel, or opaque or dry china paint—over the surface. Blow the loose color away. It sticks on the oily lines. Correct with a paintbrush, let dry, and fire like grisaille.

Workshop Hints

Vice jaws and pliers to hold a polished piece are to be covered with rubber hose, leather, or lead sheet.

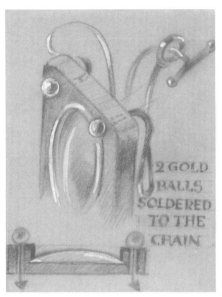

Utter simplicity: Solder two gold balls on the chain, thread it through two holes in the ivory/ebony.

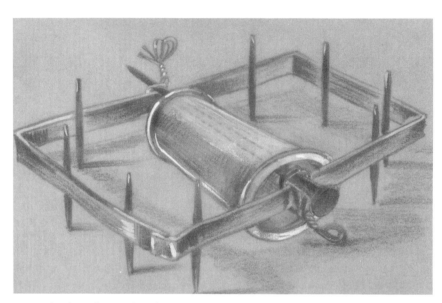

A thick nail is tied with iron wire to a trivet. The enamel-to-be has rims overhanging the inside and outside. Resting on this nail, it can easily be turned and it is safe from damage to the wetpacked enamel, which has a drop of glue on each cell. To keep in shape, the counter enamelled inside may be filled with ochre, which water will wash out after all is finished.

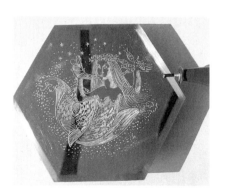 

The design is engraved on the bare metal and clear transparent fired over it. Some gold grains and painted gold complete the enamel.

Working on eight large panels at the same time:

Two identical eight inch by eight inch trivets are covered with mica. One plaque is being fired while the next dries on top of the kiln. When the glowing-hot one is removed from the kiln, a square one-quarter inch thick eight inch by eight inch iron sheet is placed onto it and remains there until the next panel is fired and removed.

Each of the ten segments of the Altar (Chapter Twenty-eight) was fired five to six times.

Any enamelled metal will keep its shape if it is fired resting on a fitted pillow of reinforced ochre.

Tables

Measurements and Weights

1 inch	25 millimeters
1 foot	0.3 meters
1 yard	0.9 meters
1 gram	.6430 dwts
1 gram	.03215 troy ounces
1 dwt	1.55517 grams
1 troy ounce	31.10348 grams
1 kilogram	32.15076 troy ounces

Troy Weights Used for Weighing Gold, Silver, and Jewels

24 grains	1 pwt
20 pwt	1 ounce
12 ounces	1 pound

Metal Melting Points

Sterling Silver	1640°F/893°C
18 carat gold	1700°F/927°C
14 carat gold	approx. 1760°F/960°C depending on alloy
Fine silver	1762°F/962°C
N-T 18 carat gold	1810°F/988°C
Fine gold	1950°F/1066°C
Copper	1981°F/1082°C

Temperatures Inside the Kiln

Dark red	approx. 1300°F/704°C
Cherry red	1400-1500°F/760-780°C
Bright cherry red	1450-1500°F/788-816°C
Light orange red	1550-1600°F/843-871°C
Orange	over 1600°F/860°C

Ring Measurements

American	European
3 1/2	14 1/2
4	15
4 1/2	15 1/2
5 3/4	16
7	17 1/2
7	18
7 3/4	18 1/2
9	19
9 1/2	19 1/2
10	20
10 3/4	20 1/2
11 1/4	21
12	12 1/2
12 1/2	22
13	22 1/2

Stones of the Month

January	Garnet, Hyacinth
February	Amethyst
March	Turmalin, Jaspis
April	Sapphire, Diamond
May	Emerald, Beryl
June	Moonstone, Chalcedony, Pearl
July	Ruby, Carneol
August	Onyx, Sardonix
September	Chrysoberyll, Peridot
October	Aquamarine, Opal
November	Topaz
December	Turquoise, Chrysopras

Zodiac Symbols

December 22 to January 21	Capricorn
January 22 to February 18	Aquarius
February 19 to March 20	Pisces
March 21 to April 20	Aries
April 21 to May 20	Taurus
May 21 to June 20	Gemini
June 21 to July 21	Cancer
July 22 to August 22	Leo
August 23 to September 22	Virgo
September 23 to October 22	Libra
October 23 to November 21	Scorpio
November 22 to December 21	Sagittarius

Finale

Do permit me just one remark: There is no instant mastery, but there is the increasing and extreme pleasure of progress and success. If you are a good enameller but know little about metal work or pewter or wood, do combine your efforts with the best of those in other trades.

Bibliography

Recommended books:

Handwrought Jewelry
by Lois E. Franke
McKnight & McKnight
Publishing Company
Bloomington, ILL

Emaux Du moyan Age Occidental
by Marie Madelaine Gauthier
Office du Livres
1972 Fribourg, Switzerland

Byzantinische Emailkunst
by Klaus Wessel
Verlag: Aurel Bongers, Recklinghausen/Germany
(available in English)

Metall
by Wilhelm Braun-Feldweg
Otto Meier Verlag, Ravensburg/Germany
(available in English)

The Art of Enamelling
by Margarete Seeler
Van Nostrand Reinhold Company, New York

Modern Pewter—Design and Techniques
by Shirley Charron
Van Nostrand Reinhold Company, New York

Where to Get Materials Needed

Gold N-T 18 carat gold sponge for painting pure gold on enamel Silver Sterling silver Solder	**T. B. Hagstoz** 709 Sansom Street Philadelphia, PA 19108

Enamels Klyr-Fire Underglaze D Scalex Sparex Guilder's metal Mica Painting colors	**Thompson Enamels** 650 Colfax Avenue Bellevue, KY 41072 (Mail to: P. O. Box 310, Newport, KY 41072) **Schauer Enamels** 1022 N.E. 68th Seattle, WA 98115

Pewter/Brass	**Oster Co.** 50 Sims Avenue Providence, RI 02909

Kilns	Paragon (Contact Thompson Enamels)

Porcelain Romain gold	Pottery supply store

Plasticene Stabilo—all Tempera	Artist supply store

Fluoron (solder flux for precious metal)	Goldsmith supply store

Copper oxide	Chemical supply store

X-ray Film	X-ray department of any hospital